I'm Saved! Now What?

The Beginning & Basics of Christian Living by Grace

Dennis M. Rokser

GRACE GOSPEL PRESS
Duluth, Minnesota

I'm Saved! Now What? The Beginning & Basics of Christian Living by Grace
© 2013 Dennis M. Rokser

All rights reserved. No portion of this publication may be reproduced, stored in a retrieval system, or transmitted in any form or by any means, electronic, mechanical, photocopy, recording, scanning, or otherwise, except as provided for by USA copyright law, without the prior written permission of the publisher.

All Scripture quotations, unless otherwise indicated, are taken from the New King James Version®. Copyright © 1982 by Thomas Nelson, Inc. Used by permission. All rights reserved.

ISBN: 978-1-939110-01-5

Library of Congress Control Number: 2013948204

GGP
Grace Gospel Press
201 W. St. Andrews Street
Duluth, MN 55803
U.S.A.
(218) 724-5914
www.gracegospelpress.com

Printed in the United States of America

CONTENTS

1. Welcome to the Family of God! 5
2. I'm Saved! Now What? 17
3. Your New Identity – "In Christ"! 23
4. Your New Spiritual Blessings in Christ! 27
5. Your New Operating Principle – God's Grace! 36
6. Your New Security – Saved and Secure Forever! 41
7. Your New Primary Motivation – The Love of Christ! 55
8. Your New Perspective of People – In Adam or In Christ! 60
9. Your New Ministry and Privilege –
    An Ambassador for Jesus Christ! 62
10. Your New Means of Communication with God –
    The Word of God & Believing Prayer! 67
11. Your New Understanding of God's Plan for You –
    The Three Tenses of Salvation! 75
12. Your New Opportunity – To Grow Spiritually! 79
13. Your New Key to Fruitfulness – Abiding in Christ! 94
14. Your New Accountability – The Coming
    Judgment Seat of Christ! 100
15. Your New Provision for When You Fail –
    Confession of Sin! 107
16. Your New Wonderful Future in Christ –
    The Blessed Hope! 113
17. Your New Beginning – In Christ! 118
    Answers to Chapter Questions 122
    Glossary of Terms & Definitions 165

Note to the Reader:

As you begin reading this book, please keep in mind that at the end of each chapter there are helpful questions for individual or group study, and the answers to those questions are at the end of the book. Also, at the back of the book there is a glossary of terms to assist you in understanding new words or phrases related to living the Christian life by grace.

Chapter 1

WELCOME TO THE FAMILY OF GOD!

If you have trusted in Jesus Christ as your personal Savior, you have been born again by God's grace. You have entered the spiritual family of God as Jesus Christ emphatically stated, "Most assuredly, I say to you, *unless one is born again, he cannot see the kingdom of God*" (John 3:3). Welcome to the forgiven and forever family of God! But I can almost hear you saying, "I'm saved! I'm forgiven! I'm going to Heaven! Now what?"

As you have now come to understand from the Scriptures, the first issue between you and God was not a change in your behavior, as needed as that might be. Instead it was an issue of spiritual birth and a change in your eternal destiny, being born again into the family of God and being guaranteed a home in Heaven. These spiritual blessings became yours through faith alone in Jesus Christ—when you believed that He is God who became a man and died for your sins and rose from the dead to give you eternal life as a free gift.

This main message of the Bible is capsulized in one of the most well-known verses in the entire Bible, John 3:16: "For God so loved the world that He gave His only begotten Son, that whoever believes in Him should not perish but have everlasting life." This tremendous promise contains four main parts that God wants everyone to know: (1) the *context* for the good news of Christ, namely, that God is holy and man is sinful and separated from God and in need of eternal life; (2) the *content* of the

I'm Saved! Now What?

good news, namely, that Christ paid for our sins by His sacrificial death and then rose from the dead; (3) the *response* to this good news that brings salvation, namely, faith alone in Christ alone; (4) the *result* of believing in Christ, namely, guaranteed eternal life. These four key components of John 3:16 are illustrated and explained below:[1]

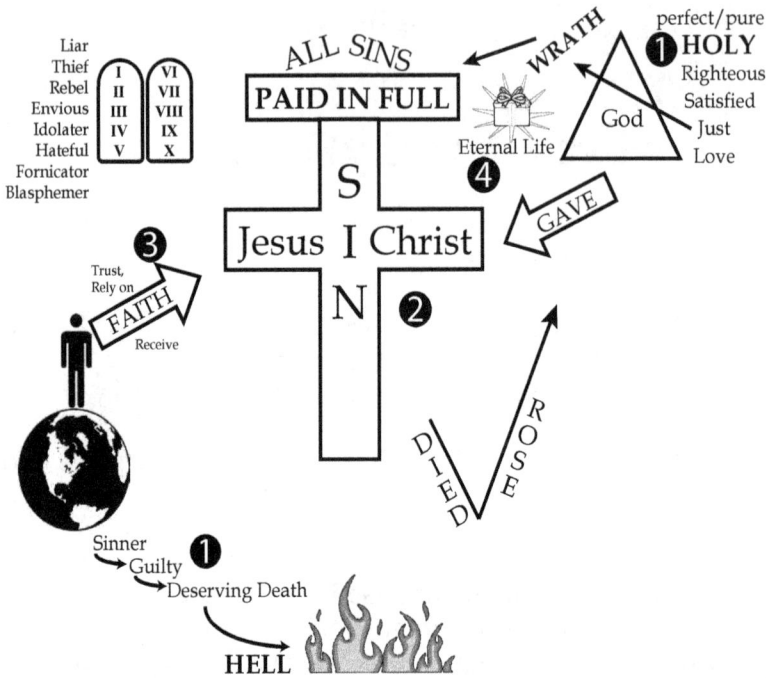

1. THE CONTEXT: *"For God"*

The promise of John 3:16 begins with a reference to "God." To understand John 3:16 a person must know who God is in His holy character and that mankind is sinful and separated from Him. According to the Bible, God is holy, righteous, and just in His character. In Psalm 99:9, it says, "For the Lord our God is

---

1. Presenting John 3:16 in terms of context, content, response, and result has proven to be a very effective method of evangelism to thousands of people, especially at fairs. To view a fuller explanation of this approach, see the video "John 3:16 Fair Diagram Explained" at the link below. www.youtube.com/watch?v=-w8s6WymPw4

Welcome to the Family of God!

holy." This means that He is perfect or pure. By necessity, this also means Heaven is a holy place. In order to correctly grasp God's holiness, He gave the law, which contains His commandments. These include commandments not to commit murder, adultery, theft, bearing false witness against one's neighbor (lying), or coveting. If we break even one of these commandments, just once, we have sinned and are considered sinners and guilty before God. Romans 3:23 concludes, "For all have sinned and fall short of the glory of God."

Because God is holy and just, there must be a consequence for breaking His laws, and the Bible declares that the penalty for sin is death. In Romans 6:23a, it says, "For the wages of sin is death." Death in the Bible does not mean nonexistence, but rather separation, like the soul and spirit of a man being separated from his body at the point of physical death. This means that mankind has earned as his spiritual "wages" death or separation from God. The "world" of sinful mankind is separated from God in His holiness by a barrier of sin. If a person never receives eternal life before he or she dies, John 3:16 states that person will "perish" forever, being eternally separated from God in Hell. This is truly bad news! But the fact of every person's sinful, spiritually dead, and condition of being separated from God must be understood in order to receive and believe the good news about Jesus Christ.

2. THE CONTENT: *"so loved the world that He gave His only begotten Son"*

No amount of good works or religious rituals could ever save you from a Hell you deserve to a Heaven you don't, since you would have to be as holy and perfect as God, and yet the Bible declares concerning our righteous deeds that "all our righteousnesses are as filthy rags" (Isa. 64:6). This is why the good news of the Gospel of salvation states that God so loved the world that He gave His only begotten Son to die to pay the penalty for the sins of all mankind that the holiness and justice of God required. Since God is now satisfied with the work of His Son in dying to pay for all of our sin, the barrier of sin between God and man has been removed in the person of the unique God-man and perfect mediator, Jesus Christ.

The good news of the Gospel states that Jesus "Christ died for our sins according the Scriptures, and that He was buried, and that He rose again the third day according to the Scriptures" (1 Cor. 15:3-4). This indeed is good news from God for helpless, hopeless, Hell-bound sinners who desperately need the only Savior God ever provided—Jesus Christ (1 Tim. 2:4-6)! And the fact that God raised His Son from the dead is proof that God's holy punishment for your sins has been forever met and satisfied with Christ's substitutionary death on the cross. He cried out on the cross, "IT IS FINISHED" (John 19:30), as all your sins were "paid in full" forever. No wonder the apostle Paul clearly writes, "I do not set aside the grace of God; for if righteousness comes through the law, then Christ died in vain" (Gal. 2:21). Yes, dear friend, if you could go to Heaven because of your good, religious works or rituals, then Christ died for nothing! But the truth is that "by grace you have been saved through faith, and that not of yourselves; it is the gift of God, not of works, lest anyone should boast" (Eph. 2:8-9).

3. THE RESPONSE: *"that whoever believes in Him"*

God's gift of eternal salvation has become personally yours the very moment you transferred your faith from a church that cannot save you, or a ritual that cannot forgive you, or attempts at a holy life which could never redeem you, and instead you placed your faith in the Lord Jesus Christ "who gave Himself for us" (Titus 2:14). Having been born again, you are now a spiritual child of God, as Galatians 3:26 declares, "For you are all sons of God through faith in Christ Jesus."

Yes, at the very moment you trusted in Jesus Christ alone, an invisible, spiritual transaction occurred between you and God. Like with your physical birth, you contributed nothing to your new spiritual birth. Why? Because God alone does all the work of saving, and He provides it to all who will simply believe in Christ on the basis of His grace or undeserved kindness. Just like your first birth, you *received* the action or the work done by another, as God Himself made you His own child when you believed. The only requirement to receive the new birth was faith alone in God's Son and His finished work, which was a choice that only you could make.

Welcome to the Family of God!

One does not become a child of God through being water baptized, whether in a fountain, lake, or river as many religions falsely teach. Nor does one become a child of God by giving— whether it be your money, time, devotion to a church, or by giving your life to Christ. Salvation comes only by *receiving* a gift from God as Christ gave His life for you (Gal. 2:20). Nor is salvation received by repenting of your sins, though admittedly we are all sinners as Christ died for all your sins—past, present, and future. Nor is salvation yours by asking Christ into your life, though He comes in when you believe in Him for salvation (Gal. 4:4-6).[2] The sole requirement of faith alone in Christ alone must be clarified because there are many people today who claim to be born again who have prayed a prayer, signed a card, or made a commitment to Christ but have never understood the Gospel and trusted in Christ's work alone to save them. They are like those spoken of by Jesus Christ:

> Not everyone who says to Me, "Lord, Lord," shall enter the kingdom of heaven, but he who does the will of My Father in heaven. Many will say to Me in that day, "Lord, Lord, have we not prophesied in Your name, cast out demons in Your name, and done many wonders in Your name?" And then I will declare to them, "I never knew you; depart from Me, you who practice lawlessness!" (Matt. 7:21-23)

What is "the will of My Father in Heaven"? It is simply to "believe on the Lord Jesus Christ, and you will be saved" (Acts 16:31). In Matthew 7:21-23, observe how these religious individuals claim to believe in the "Lord" but they still rely on their religious works to gain favor before God (they "prophesied," "cast out demons," and did "many wonders"), while they professed to be doing all these things in Christ's "name." Yet, what will be Jesus Christ's verdict and reply to them on the day they stand before Him? It will sadly be, "I never knew you"! This means they never had a personal relationship with Jesus Christ by God's grace because they sought salvation through faith in

---

2. See Dennis M. Rokser, *Don't Ask Jesus into Your Heart: A Biblical Answer to the Question: "What Must I Do to Be Saved?"* (Duluth, MN: Grace Gospel Press, 2014).

Christ *plus* their works, instead of through faith alone in Christ alone. For the Scripture teaches, "But as many as *received Him*, to them He gave the right to become *children of God*, to those who *believe in His name: who were born*, not of blood, nor of the will of the flesh, nor of the will of man, but *of God*" (John 1:12-13).

These verses make it clear that the new birth comes by receiving Jesus Christ as Savior. And how does one receive Jesus Christ? It occurs when we "believe in His name" (which represents who Christ is and what He has done). The new birth is the result of simply believing the Gospel!

4. THE RESULT: *"should not perish but have eternal life."*

According to Jesus Christ's promise in John 3:16, the result of believing in Him as your Savior is that you now possess eternal life, which goes on forever, and you will not perish. The sole reason eternal life can be assured and gauranteed to you is because it rests solely upon Jesus Christ's finished work and faithfulness rather than your own insufficient works. If you could still perish after believing in Christ and receiving eternal life as a result of sin in your life or insufficient good works, then Christ's promise here would not be true. You would not have "eternal" life, which goes on forever and you would still "perish." Yet according to the Bible, if you have already trusted in Christ alone for your salvation, then you have already received eternal life at the moment you believed, and you are guaranteed that you will not be condemned at any point in the future. Thus, Jesus Christ promised later in John 5:24, "Most assuredly, I say to you, he who hears My word and believes in Him who sent Me has everlasting life, and shall not come into judgment, but has passed from death into life." According to this promise, if you have believed, you have already passed from death into life (in the past), and now have everlasting life (in the present), and shall not come into God's judgment (in the future). What assurance God's Word and Christ's finished work provide!

So if you have been born again, why don't you stop right now and thank God for providing eternal salvation to you as a free gift? Why not thank Jesus Christ for having loved you by dying on the cross for your sins and rising from the dead to per-

Welcome to the Family of God!

sonally give you eternal life apart from your works? Like the old hymn of the faith says, this is "Amazing Grace"!

> Amazing grace, how sweet the sound
> that saved a wretch like me!
> I once was lost but now am found,
> was blind but now I see.
> T'was grace that caused my heart to fear [the judgment of God for my sins],
> and grace my fears relieved [when I understood that Christ died for me].
> How precious did that grace appear,
> the hour I first believed!

However, if you have never been saved by God's grace, you need to recognize that you are a helpless, hopeless, Hell-bound sinner before a holy God and that you are unable to save yourself by your good works or religious rituals. Yet God loves you and wants to save you and give you eternal life. To make eternal salvation possible, Jesus Christ left the glories of Heaven to die for your sins on the cross and take the full weight of the punishment you deserved before God. This perfectly satisfied the holy Judge of Heaven so that He is willing to forgive you and grant you eternal life as a free gift because Jesus Christ paid for it with His shed blood. Jesus Christ then conquered death through His resurrection in order for this gift of salvation to become yours. But you must personally receive Jesus Christ through faith in Him alone. Are you ready to accept God's gift right now by trusting in Christ as your Savior?

> For God so loved the world that He gave His only begotten Son, that *whoever believes in Him should not perish but have everlasting life.* For God did not send His Son into the world to condemn the world, but that the world through Him might be saved. *He who believes in Him is not condemned; but he who does not believe is condemned already, because he has not believed in the name of the only begotten Son of God.* (John 3:16-18)

Don't put off this destiny-determining decision. "For He says: 'In an acceptable time I have heard you, and in the day of salvation I have helped you.' *Behold, now is the accepted time; behold, now is the day of salvation"* (2 Cor. 6:2). And once Jesus Christ is received by faith and becomes yours, God personally says to you: "And this is the testimony: that God has given us eternal life, and this life is in His Son. *He who has the Son has life; he who does not have the Son of God does not have life. These things I have written to you who believe in the name of the Son of God, that you may know that you have eternal life"* (1 John 5:11-13). Dear friend, because God said it (in His Word), and Christ did it (when He died for you and rose again), if you believe it, that settles it. You can know beyond a shadow of a doubt that you are saved forever, regardless of your feelings, for God cannot lie (Titus 1:2)!

Welcome to the Family of God!

Chapter 1 Questions

1. What is the first issue between a sinner and God?

2. What verse in the Bible capsulizes the main message of the Bible?

3. Who is the subject of John 3:16? What is the context of John 3:16?

4. What does it mean that God is holy?

5. What did God give to man to express His holy commands?

6. What is the wage or penalty for sin?

7. Can your good works or religious rituals ever save you from Hell? Why or why not?

8. Regarding the content of John 3:16, who does John 3:16 tell us about?

9. Describe Jesus Christ. Is he a God or a man?

10. For what purpose did Jesus Christ die?

11. What is the proof that God accepted the substitutionary death of Christ as a complete payment for our sins?

12. What did Jesus mean when He cried out on the cross, "It is finished"?

13. What is the only correct way to respond to the Gospel?

14. By what means is a person not saved or born again?

15. What is "grace"?

16. Do people contribute anything to their spiritual birth? Would it be grace if you contributed some action or work to be born again?

17. Is salvation an earned reward or a free gift?

Welcome to the Family of God!

18. The one condition to receive the gift of salvation really needs to be clarified. Why is this needed so badly for so many people?

19. What is the result of believing the Gospel?

20. When exactly does a person become born again and receive the gift of eternal life?

21. Will the believer in Christ ever come into God's condemnation in the future? Why or why not?

22. How should the person who has received eternal life as a free gift logically respond toward God and Jesus Christ?

23. If eternal salvation is this simple, what ultimately condemns a person to Hell? For help, see John 3:17-18.

24. Can a person know with 100-percent certainty that he/she has eternal life upon believing in Him alone? For help, see 1 John 5:11-13.

25. Do you know for sure that you have eternal life? If not, why not settle the issue right now? Why not put your name in John 3:16 and believe the Gospel for yourself?

    For God so loved _____, that He gave His only begotten Son to die for _____ and be raised from the dead, that if _____ believes in Him, _____ should not perish in Hell, but _____ will now and forever possess eternal life. Is this not good news from God to you?!

Chapter 2

I'M SAVED! NOW WHAT?

This is a vital question, which the remainder of this book will now answer from the Word of God. Since every child of God needs divine direction from the Lord and a solid, spiritual foundation for their new life in Christ, it will be of greater benefit to you to read this book *carefully*, *prayerfully*, and even *repeatedly* as necessary. But it is wonderful to now know that God states without apology:

> Therefore, *if anyone is in Christ, he is a new creation*; old things have passed away; behold, all things have become new. (2 Cor. 5:17)

Yes, God states emphatically that you have become a new creation in Christ! And in this booklet we will explore some of the "new" spiritual realities that are yours because of your eternal, personal relationship with Jesus Christ. But let's clarify something immediately lest you be confused from the onset. When 2 Corinthians 5:17 says, "old things have passed away; behold, all things have become new," it is not teaching that all of your sinful practices have now ceased. Nor is it stating that all your wrong thoughts and beliefs have instantaneously changed (I wish this were true but it is not). Instead these many issues of your daily Christian living will only be addressed and changed through the ongoing process of spiritual growth as you repeatedly study and receive the Word of God by faith and apply it in your life.

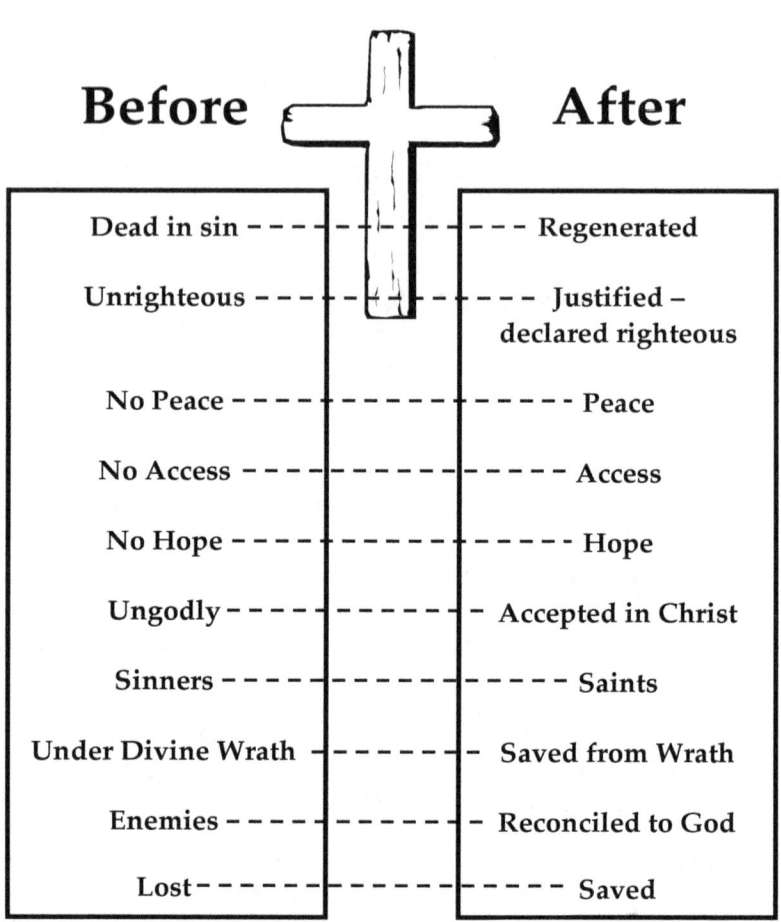

Keep in mind that many of the old leaves of autumn only fall off when the new buds of spring eventually come in. This principle of spiritual growth is important to clarify at the beginning of this booklet since a person's assurance of eternal salvation is sometimes undermined by those who twist or misunderstand 2 Corinthians 5:17. Some misinterpret this verse and the phrase "all things have become new" to be a reference to the believer's *daily walk or practice* (which still needs much transformation) instead of his *new position in Christ* (which is unchanging and settled forever). They say in effect, "If you are still living with sin in your life you were never really saved." However, this verse clearly states that you now have a new identity (you are "in Christ") and that "all things have become new" in terms of your new position, possessions, and privileges in Christ.

Chapter 2 Questions

1. Since every child of God needs a solid spiritual foundation, what is suggested that you do?

2. What does 2 Corinthians 5:15 state is true of all believers in Christ?

3. What does 2 Corinthians 5:17 mean?

4. What does 2 Corinthians 5:17 not mean?

5. What will be necessary to address these issues in your Christian life?

6. Why is it necessary to clarify 2 Corinthians 5:17?

7. Observing the chart in this chapter, what things were true of you before you were saved, and what is true of you now because you are "in Christ"?

8. Using the Glossary of Terms and Definitions at the end of this book, look up the meaning of the various blessings you have in Christ as stated in the chart in this chapter (and discuss them in your study group).

9. If a believer is still living or struggling with sin in his/her life, does this mean that person was never saved or born again?

10. What does "in Christ" refer to? And what is "all things become new" referring to?

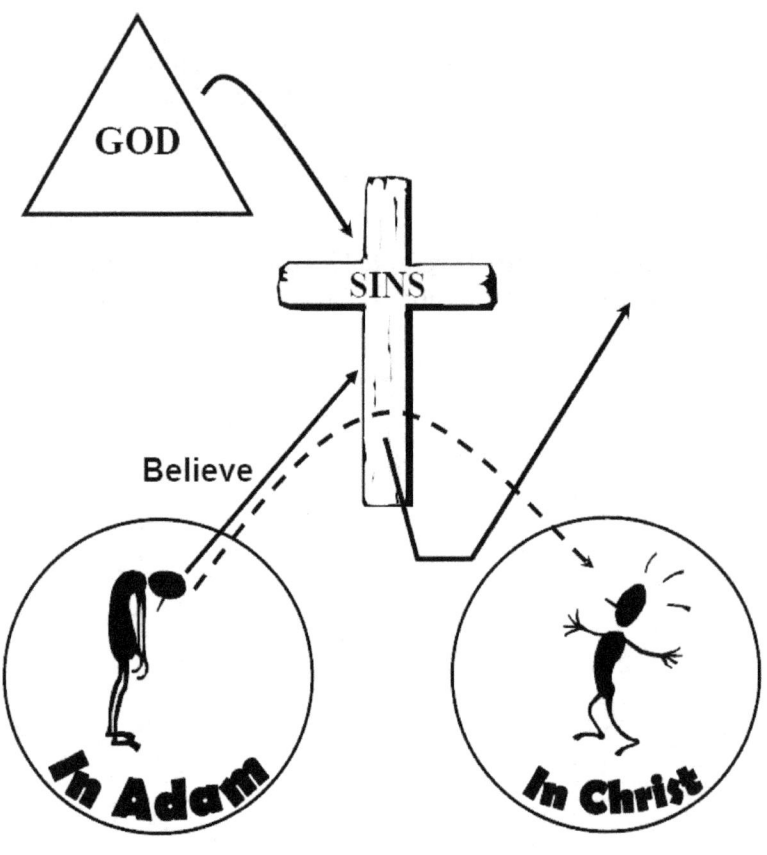

Chapter 3

YOUR NEW IDENTITY—"IN CHRIST"!

Did you realize that before you were saved from Hell by God's grace, you were viewed by God as identified with the first man "Adam" and the old creation as an unregenerate sinner who was spiritually dead and separated from God (Rom. 5:12-21; Eph. 2:1-3)? You were "in Adam" and part of the "Adam's family" (1 Cor. 15:22); and as such you were "without Christ," "having no hope and without God in the world" (Eph. 2:12). So who and what made the difference in your life? "But now *in Christ Jesus* you who once were far off *have been brought near by the blood of Christ*" (Eph. 2:13).

Yes, dear believer, God sees and relates to you "now in Christ Jesus" and you have been brought near to God "by the blood of Christ." The "blood of Christ" refers to His sacrificial death on the cross when He died for you to completely pay the penalty for your sins that God's perfect justice required (Rom. 6:23). Observe again that it was not a church, a ritual, or a commitment on your part that brought you near to God—it was the blood of Jesus Christ! Thus, God will now and forever relate to you as one who has been identified with, or placed into, His Son. You are "in Christ"! Thus, you also need to begin seeing yourself as God sees you—as a new creation in Christ! He loves you and accepts you just as He does His very own Beloved Son, Jesus Christ, for you are now and forever in Him and all of this is "to the praise of the glory of His grace, by which He has made us accepted in the Beloved" (Eph. 1:6).

> By nature and by practice far,
> How very far from God!
> Yet now by grace brought near to Him,
> Through faith in Jesus' blood.
>
> Near, so very near to God,
> nearer I could not be;
> for in the person of His Son,
> I'm just as near as He.
>
> Dear, so very dear to God,
> dearer I could not be;
> for in the person of His Son,
> I'm just as dear as He.
>
> So dear, so very dear to God,
> More dear I cannot be;
> The love wherewith He loves the Son,
> Such is His love to me.[1]

---

1. Adapted from the hymn written by Horatius Bonar, "A Mind at Perfect Peace."

Chapter 3 Questions

1. Before you were saved, how did God view you in terms of your position or identity?

2. What spiritual realities were true of you before you were "in Christ"?

3. Who and what made the difference in your life spiritually?

4. What does the "blood of Christ" refer to?

5. As a believer, how does God relate to you right now and for the rest of eternity?

6. According to Ephesians 1:6, how does God "accept" you?

7. According to Ephesians 1:6, your incredible position in Christ magnifies and praises what aspect of God?

8. What does the poem at the end of the chapter mean to you personally?

9. What kind of positive transformation will occur if believers begin to truly grasp how God now views them in Christ?

10. Group discussion assignment: Look up the following verses and state what you observe about your position or identity in Christ. (Use the glossary of terms and definitions as needed.)

   a. 1 Corinthians 15:22

   b. Ephesians 1:3

   c. Ephesians 1:6

   d. Ephesians 1:7

   e. Ephesians 1:13

   f. Ephesians 2:4-7

   g. Ephesians 2:8-9

   h. Ephesians 2:10

   i. Ephesians 2:11-13

Chapter 4

YOUR NEW SPIRITUAL BLESSINGS IN CHRIST!

Just as a child born into a king's family may be blessed with many physical blessings and privileges because of his birth and relationship to the king, so every child of God is now "in Christ" and is the recipient of all "spiritual blessings" in Christ Jesus.

> Blessed be the God and Father of our Lord Jesus Christ, *who has blessed us with every spiritual blessing in the heavenly places in Christ.* (Eph. 1:3)

It is helpful to observe that every believer in Christ (not just some) has already been blessed (as a past reality) with every spiritual blessing (not every physical one) in the heavenly places (the believer's new realm of existence) in Christ (because of their identity or union with Christ). This is also why God states that "you are complete in Him" (Col. 2:10). Just like a child is born complete with ten fingers, ten toes, two arms, and two legs at the moment of physical birth but just needs now to grow, so every child of God is born again and already fully blessed in Christ, though still needing to grow spiritually. This is important to remember because there are those false teachers today who will entice you to believe that though you have been saved, you still need "something more" from God like receiving the ability to speak in tongues, or be slain by the Spirit, or achieve some ecstatic, mystical experience. Some may also teach that God now wants you to be prospered with all physical wealth and health, if you would only "claim it in the name of Jesus." However, if this is true, why were Jesus Christ (Luke 9:58) and the apostles financially poor (1 Cor. 4:8-14) and other godly believers physically sick (Phil. 2:25-30) while serving the Lord? Beware of this trap of Satan!

What are some of the spiritual blessings that you now have "in Christ"? Consider the following partial list of what is yours and every believer's in Christ. You can joyfully say based on the authority of God's Word:

1. My salvation is fully accomplished (John 19:30).
2. I have eternal life as a present possession (John 5:24; 6:47; 1 John 5:11-13).
3. I have Jesus Christ as my present possession (1 John 5:12).
4. I know personally the one, true God (John 17:3; 1 John 2:3; 5:20).
5. I have been saved from Hell by His grace (Eph. 2:1-10).
6. I have been justified by His grace (Titus 3:7).
7. I have passed from spiritual death into spiritual life (John 5:24; 1 John 3:14).
8. I have been made alive spiritually by God (Eph. 2:1, 5; Col. 2:13).
9. I have been made fit for Heaven which is my future destiny (Col. 1:12).
10. I have the forgiveness of all my sins—past, present, and future (Eph. 1:7; Col. 1:14).
11. My sins have been taken away (John 1:29; Heb. 9:26; 1 John 3:5).
12. My sins have been completely purged (Heb. 1:3).
13. My sins will never be remembered by God (Heb. 8:12; 10:17).
14. I have been washed from all my sins (1 Cor. 6:11; Titus 3:5; Rev. 1:5).

15. I have been reconciled forever to God (2 Cor. 5:18-19; Col. 1:20).
16. I have been made near to God by the blood of Christ (Eph. 2:13).
17. I have been redeemed through His blood (Eph. 1:7; Col. 1:14; 1 Peter 1:18-19).
18. I have been bought with the price of the blood of Christ (1 Cor. 6:20; 7:23).
19. I have been delivered from the power of darkness (Col. 1:13).
20. I have been delivered from the wrath of God to come (1 Thess. 1:10).
21. I will not come into future condemnation or punishment by God (John 5:24; Rom. 8:1).
22. I am a child of God (John 1:12; Rom. 8:16; Gal. 3:26; 1 John 3:1-2).
23. I belong to Jesus Christ (Gal. 3:29; 5:24).
24. I have obtained an eternal inheritance (Eph. 1:11, 14; Heb. 1:14; 9:15; 1 Peter 1:4).
25. I am a new creation in Christ (2 Cor. 5:17; Eph. 2:10; 4:24; Col. 3:10).
26. I have been renewed and regenerated by the Holy Spirit (John 3:7; Titus 3:5).
27. I am accepted and highly favored in the Beloved One (Eph. 1:6 cf. Matt. 3:17).
28. I have been seated in heavenly places with Christ (Eph. 2:6).
29. I am a priest who can offer spiritual sacrifices to God (Heb. 13:15-16; 1 Peter 2:5, 9; Rev. 1:6; 5:10; 20:6).
30. I am privileged to have fellowship with the Father and with the Son (1 John 1:3).
31. Jesus Christ dwells in me (John 6:56; Gal. 2:20; 1 John 3:24; 4:12-16).

32. I am in Christ (John 14:20; 2 Cor. 5:17).
33. The Spirit of God dwells in me (Rom. 8:9; 1 Cor. 3:16; Eph. 2:21-22).
34. My body is the temple of the Holy Spirit (1 Cor. 6:19).
35. I have been blessed with the gift and pledge of the Holy Spirit (2 Cor. 1:22; Gal. 4:6; Eph. 1:13-14).
36. God predestined me to be conformed to Christ's image (Rom. 8:29; Eph. 1:5, 11).
37. I have already been glorified according to God's mind and purpose (Rom. 8:30).
38. I am eternally secure in God's love (Rom. 8:35-39).
39. I am chosen in Christ (Eph. 1:4; Col. 3:12; 1 Thess. 1:4; 1 Peter 2:9; Rev. 17:14).
40. I am complete in Christ (Col. 2:10).
41. I am beloved of God (Col. 3:12; 2 Thess. 2:13).
42. I am a sheep in His flock (Luke 12:32; Heb. 13:20; 1 Peter 2:25).
43. I am a member of His Body (1 Cor. 10:17; 12:27; Eph. 3:6; 4:25; 5:30).
44. I am a stone in His building (Eph. 2:20-22; Heb. 3:6; 1 Peter 2:5).
45. I am a branch in the Vine—Jesus Christ (John 15:1-7).
46. I was baptized by the Holy Spirit into Jesus Christ (Rom. 6:3; 1 Cor. 12:12-13; Gal. 3:27).
47. I was identified with Christ in His death (Rom. 6:3-6, 8-11; 2 Cor. 5:14; Col. 2:12, 20; 3:3).
48. I was identified with Christ in His resurrection (Rom. 6:5, 8, 11; 2 Cor. 5:15; Gal. 2:20; Col. 2:12; 3:1).

49. I died to the sin nature in Christ (Rom. 6:2).
50. I am alive to God in Christ (Rom. 6:11, 13; Gal. 2:19, 20).
51. Christ is my life (Phil. 1:21; Col. 3:4).
52. I can walk in newness of life (Rom. 6:4).
53. I can serve in newness of the Spirit (Rom. 7:6).
54. I can live to righteousness (1 Peter 2:24).
55. I died to the Law (Rom. 7:4; Gal. 2:19).
56. I am delivered from the Law (Rom. 7:6).
57. I am not under law but under grace for sanctification (Rom. 6:14).
58. I am not of the world though still in it (John 17:14, 16).
59. The world is crucified to me (Gal. 6:14).
60. I am crucified to the world (Gal. 6:14).
61. I am set apart or sanctified positionally in Christ (1 Cor. 1:2; 6:11; Heb. 10:10; Jude 1).
62. I am a saint—set apart to God (1 Cor. 1:2; Phil. 1:1; Col. 1:2; Rom. 1:7).
63. I am perfected forever (Heb. 10:14).
64. I am a citizen of Heaven (Phil. 3:20).
65. I am a stranger and pilgrim who is no longer at home in this world (Heb.11:13; 1 Pet. 2:11).
66. I have all things that pertain to life and godliness (2 Peter 1:3).
67. I have grace to help in time of need (Heb. 4:16).
68. I have an unfailing Intercessor who prays for me (Heb. 7:25; 9:24; Rom. 8:34).
69. I have a righteous Advocate with the Father for times when I sin (1 John 2:1).
70. I have peace with God (Rom. 5:1).

71. I belong to a sovereign God who now works all things together for my good (Rom. 8:28).
72. I am His workmanship (Eph. 2:10).
73. I am kept by the power of God (1 Peter 1:5).
74. I am preserved in Jesus Christ (Jude 1).
75. My name is forever written in Heaven (Luke 10:20).
76. I am more than a conqueror, even a super-conqueror in Christ (Rom. 8:37).
77. I have victory through Christ over death (1 Cor. 15:57).
78. I have a glorious future to look forward to (Rom. 8:18; 2 Thess. 2:14).
79. I have been given eternal comfort and good hope through grace (2 Thess. 2:16).
80. I have a place reserved in Heaven for me (John 14:2, 3; 1 Peter 1:4).
81. I will not be hurt by the second death, namely, eternal Hell (Rev. 2:11; 20:6).
82. I will not ever have my name blotted out of the book of life (Rev. 3:5).
83. I will be with my God forever (Rev. 21:3-4).

These spiritual blessings (and many more) are the present possession of all believers from the very moment they believe the Gospel and are placed into an eternal relationship with Christ by the Holy Spirit (1 Cor. 12:12-13). In addition, these spiritual blessings are true of you whether you realize it or not. Unfortunately, many believers are ignorant or untaught about their spiritual riches in Christ. Thus, they live daily like spiritual paupers instead of saved princes in the family of God because of their ignorance of their spiritual riches in Christ.

This problem is similar to a lady by the name of Hetty Green who is known in American history as "America's Greatest Miser." Yet, when she died in 1916, she left an estate valued at $100 million. That was a lot of money in 1916! It is said that Hetty was so miserly that she ate cold oatmeal because she thought it was too expensive to heat the water to warm it. Her son had a severe leg injury, but because she delayed so long to find a free clinic, his leg had to be amputated. Eventually, she had an attack of apoplexy (bleeding within internal organs) which hastened her own death, while arguing over the merits of skim milk because it was cheaper than whole milk. Though Hetty was very wealthy, she lived like a beggar because she did not understand or utilize her financial resources. Will the same be said spiritually of you in your Christian life? Will you access by faith your spiritual riches in Christ (Rom. 5:2) and live your life consistent with your position in Christ (Eph. 4:1)? May you grow in your understanding of your new position and possessions in Christ. This is a great reason to begin studying your Bible; for only in God's Word will you read about your spiritual wealth and assets in Christ.

Chapter 4 Questions

1. According to Ephesians 1:3, what is now true of every believer "in Christ"?

2. According to Colossians 2:10, what also is true of those "in Christ"?

3. How can the illustration of a newborn baby assist you to grasp what Ephesians 1:3 and Colossians 2:10 mean as they relate to your possessions in Christ and spiritual growth?

4. What does a failure to understand your completeness in Christ lead people to falsely teach or believe?

5. How do Luke 9:58, 1 Corinthians 4:8-14, and Philippians 2:25-30 prove the sufficiency of your spiritual position and blessings in Christ?

6. This chapter has a partial listing of the believer's blessings or possessions in Christ. Look up some (next page), or all the verses if you have time, in your Bible. You may use the Glossary of Terms and Definitions at the back of this book to understand the meaning of some of these biblical words.

Your New Spiritual Blessings in Christ

7. Read out loud this list as you marvel at the riches of God's grace to you. If this is a group study, you can have each person in turn read out loud the blessings on the list until every blessing has been stated.

8. When do these spiritual blessings become the believer's present and eternal possession?

9. Spiritual ignorance is not bliss but a serious blunder for every child of God. Does God want believers in Christ to be ignorant of their position and their spiritual blessings in Christ?

10. To understand better what God wants for you as a new believer, read Ephesians 1:3, followed by 1:15-23. Also, God wants you to live with the awareness of your blessings in Christ Jesus each day. Read Ephesians 4:1-3.

11. Where will you read and learn about your riches in Christ?

12. Why not end this session by pausing to praise and thank God in prayer for some or all of these wonderful blessings in Christ that He has given you because of the finished work of Christ and the riches of His amazing grace.

Chapter 5

YOUR NEW OPERATING PRINCIPLE—GOD'S GRACE!

Grace (*charis*) in its primary definition refers to God's unmerited kindness or blessing. God deals with us in incredible grace because of who He is and what Jesus Christ has done for us, not because of who we are or what we have done for Him. This grace approach is totally foreign to our natural thinking (Isaiah 55:8-11) in which we seek to earn, deserve, or merit God's blessings because of our religious works or rituals. Thus, we are prone to think (as reinforced by religion) that salvation, Heaven, and God's blessings are an earned reward for our works, instead of an undeserved gift because of what Christ did for us on Calvary. Thus, God's grace approach versus man's merit or works approach are contrasted in various passages of Scripture such as the following:

> And if by grace, then it is no longer of works; otherwise grace is no longer grace. But if it is of works, it is no longer grace; otherwise work is no longer work. (Rom. 11:6)

> Now to him who works, the wages are not counted as grace but as debt. But to him who does not work but believes on Him who justifies the ungodly, his faith is accounted for righteousness. (Rom. 4:4-5)

Your New Operating Principle

> For by grace you have been saved through faith, and that not of yourselves; it is the gift of God, not of works, lest anyone should boast. (Eph. 2:8-9)

The only human response that is consistent with God's grace (an undeserved gift) is faith in Jesus Christ alone. When you trusted in Christ as your Savior you did not try to earn salvation by your good works; instead, you relied on the finished work of another—Jesus Christ! But it is one thing to get a glimpse of understanding of God's grace at your salvation; it's quite another to get established firmly in an understanding of God's grace in all phases of your Christian life.

Grace means that God does not love you any more or less based on anything you do—whether good or bad. This is because grace is undeserved kindness and blessing from God. It is not based upon you but upon God, as He is "the God of all grace" (1 Peter 5:10). And God's grace is personally appropriated by faith in Christ alone (Rom. 3:28). Thus, you now have constant access to God's grace (Rom. 5:2), and you are to grow in grace (2 Peter 3:18), serve by grace (1 Cor. 15:10), and become established with grace (Heb. 13:9). In every trial and painful affliction you face, the Lord reminds you, "My grace is sufficient for you" (2 Cor. 12:9). Isn't this good to know?

As a believer, the Lord now wants you to get established and grow in grace? This comes only by reading, hearing, studying, and believing the Word of God (Acts 20:32). God must transform your thinking through His Word. I would highly recommend, even if you have some knowledge of the Bible already, that you start reading the Scriptures in the Gospel of John, observing in particular all the verses that guarantee eternal life by simply believing in Christ alone. Then I would encourage you to read Paul's letter to the Romans and continue reading thereafter right on through the rest of the New Testament. As you read, there will be many things that you do not understand and that will require further study or explanation. You will not understand everything at once. However, be sure to enjoy what you *do* understand and feel free to underline verses in your Bible so you can find them at a later time. Finally, let me recommend that you go online to watch or listen to the messages titled, "It Is Finished (John 19:30)"[1] and "The Wonder of Calvary."[2]

If you have very little knowledge of the Bible, I would like to recommend an excellent book titled, *By this Name,*[3] which will give you a foundational understanding of the message of the Bible from creation through the death and resurrection of Jesus Christ. In doing so, it will put many pieces of the puzzle together in your thinking. I cannot recommend this too highly!

Also, the booklet titled, *John 3:16 Illustrated,* is an excellent resource to read through to become more established in the Gospel of salvation in Jesus Christ.

---

1. www.sermonaudio.com/sermoninfo.asp?SID=42007121844
2. www.sermonaudio.com/sermoninfo.asp?SID=41209112129
3. us.goodseed.com/products/By-this-Name-%28English%29.html
4. www.gracegospelpress.org/free-downloads/

Chapter 5 Questions

1. What is the primary definition of "grace" (*charis*)?

2. Why does God deal with man in such amazing grace?

3. Look up and read Isaiah 55:8-11. Do we naturally think according to God's grace?

4. What observations can you make when reading Romans 11:6, Romans 4:4-5, and Ephesians 2:8-9?

5. Go back and read Romans 4:5 and Ephesians 2:8-9, along with Acts 10:43, 13:38-39, 16:30-31, and Romans 3:28. What is the only human response consistent with God's grace?

6. How is God described in 1 Peter 5:10?

I'm Saved! Now What?

7. Look up the following verses and observe what each one teaches you regarding God's grace (Romans 5:1-2; 2 Peter 3:18; 1 Cor. 15:10; Hebrews 13:9; 2 Cor. 12:7-9).

8. Look up Revelation 1:3; Romans 10:17; 2 Timothy 2:15; and Acts 20:32. How does a believer become established in the truths of God's grace?

9. What are some recommendations when a believer first starts reading the Bible?

10. What can you learn about God's grace and prayer from Hebrews 4:14-16?

Chapter 6

YOUR NEW SECURITY—
SAVED AND SECURE FOREVER!

Dear believer in Christ, it is self-evident that children grow best in a home where they know they are loved unconditionally and are secure in their relationship with their parents. This same truth applies in the spiritual realm. God wants every one of His blood-bought, born-again children to know that they are unconditionally loved by Him and are eternally secure in their family relationship with God. Thus, the Bible is replete with many verses which clearly underscore the truth that all believers shall never perish forever and are kept saved eternally by God's grace and power. The assurance of this great scriptural truth is the birthright of every believer in Christ. Consider the following verses.

1. God declares that you are now *a child of God forever*. "But as many as received Him, *to them He gave the right to become children of God*, to those who believe in His name." (John 1:12)

No matter how hard you try, you cannot undo your physical birth. It is a once-for-all occurrence that can never be repeated or undone. The same is true with a believer's spiritual birth. It is a once-for-all, non-repeatable birth that cannot be undone since it is fully accomplished by God. But *entering the family of God* at a moment of time when you trust in Christ as Savior must be kept distinct from the believer's *daily fellowship with God*. Entrance into the family of God occurs only once, while fellowship with the Lord is to occur daily, step by step, and moment by moment as you learn to walk by faith. However, sin in the life of the child of God breaks fellowship with God (1 John 1:3-7) and displeases Him. Sin also brings God's loving discipline upon that believer (Hebrews 12:5-11) if he refuses to acknowledge and confess his sin (1 John 1:9-10). Nevertheless, the believer remains a child of God because Jesus Christ already paid for all of our sins (Heb. 10:10-14) and God has already positionally forgiven us completely (Col. 2:13). Yet personal sin affects our *daily fellowship with God*.

If you are a parent you can certainly relate to these scriptural principles. From the first day of their birth to the present, your children have been and will always be part of your family. They have your DNA. They will always be your children whether they obey you or rebel against you. Why? It is because they have been birthed by you. Yet, when your children have rebelled against your will and direction for them, you have become displeased with them — the fellowship has been broken until some admission occurs.

In the same way, every child of God has been born again at the moment they accepted the Gospel by faith. They now have the DNA of God. They have been spiritually birthed by God Himself. Their standing before God is settled forever — they are children of God regardless of their daily behavior or performance. It is all by God's grace that they are and will always be children of God! However, when believers choose to sin and disobey their Heavenly Father, they break fellowship with Him. This also displeases the Lord. But they still remain a child of God in the family of God. Why? It is because they have been "born again" by God Himself. Praise the Lord!

Your New Security

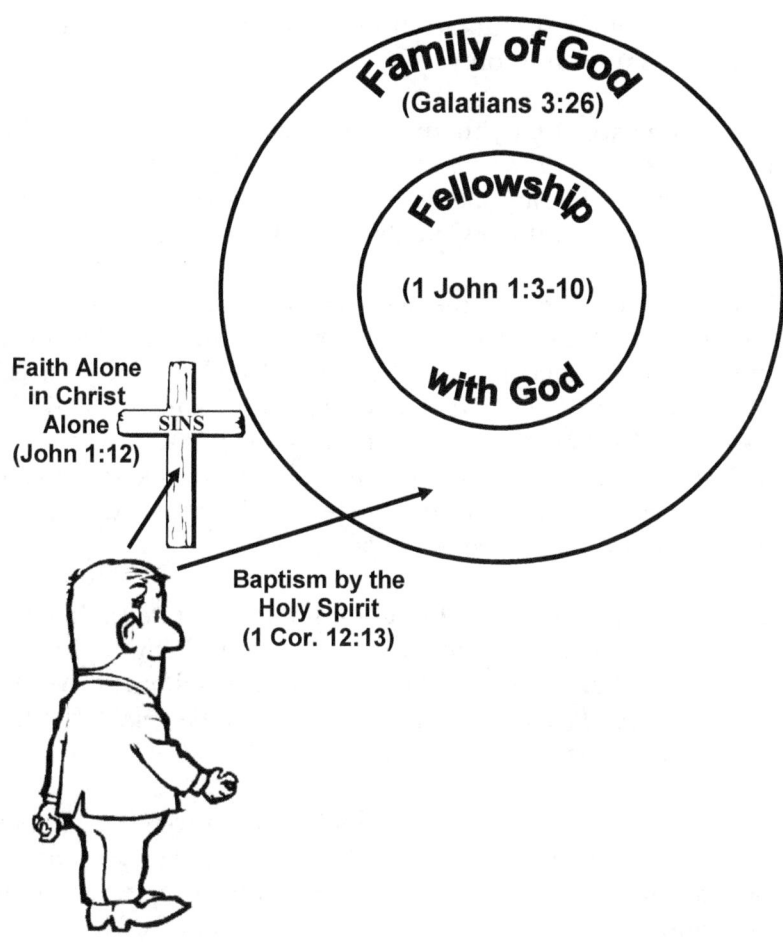

2. God promises you that every believer in Christ *presently possesses eternal life.* "For God so loved the world that He gave His only begotten Son, that *whoever believes in Him should not perish but have everlasting life.*" (John 3:16)

The very moment sinners place their faith in Jesus Christ alone, they "have [present tense] everlasting life." How long does everlasting life last for? Forever! Thus, your new birth cannot be undone by your sin, unfaithfulness, or carnality as you have eternal life now and forever.

3. God declares that you either presently *possess eternal life or else you have never possessed* it. "He who *believes in the Son has everlasting life;* and he who *does not believe the Son shall not see life*, but the wrath of God abides on him." (John 3:36)

The contrast is between the one "who believes in the Son" versus "he who does not believe the Son." The first has "everlasting life" which lasts forever. The latter "shall not see [eternal] life" — whether it be for five, ten, or twenty years. Instead, the "wrath of God abides on him" because he has never believed in Jesus Christ as his Savior. Thus, either you have received eternal life the moment you trusted in the finished work of Jesus Christ or you have never possessed it!

4. God has promised that you are guaranteed *never to come into future condemnation*. "Most assuredly, I say to you, he who hears My word and believes in Him who sent Me [1] *has everlasting life*, and [2] *shall not come into judgment*, but has passed from death into life." (John 5:24)

Every believer has "everlasting life" and is promised by God never to "come into judgment." If you could lose your salvation through sin, unfaithfulness, carnality, or apostasy, then you would come into future condemnation and God's promise would be a lie! But God cannot lie, and you can be assured of His promises because you have already "passed from [spiritual] death into [spiritual] life" the moment you were born again.

5. God has promised that you will *never be cast out of His family*. "And Jesus said to them, 'I am the bread of life. He who comes to Me *shall never hunger*, and he who believes in Me *shall never thirst*. But I said to you that you have seen Me and yet do not believe. All that the Father gives Me will come to Me, and the one who comes to Me *I will by no means cast out*.'" (John 6:35-37)

Your New Security

If you have come to Christ by faith in Him alone, God promises that He will never cast you out. The Greek words translated, "by no means" (*ou mē*), refer to something that will never occur under any conditions or circumstances and are often translated "never" in the Bible. Didn't God know fully what He was getting when He saved you? Yet He still accepted you in Christ according to the riches of His grace (Eph. 1:6)!

6. God has promised that in Christ you will *never be lost again*. "For I have come down from heaven, not to do My own will, but the will of Him who sent Me. This is the will of the Father who sent Me, that of all He has given Me *I should lose nothing*, but should raise it up at the last day. And this is the will of Him who sent Me, that everyone who sees the Son and believes in Him may have *everlasting life*; and *I will raise him up at the last day*." (John 6:38-40)

Once again Jesus Christ guarantees the eternal salvation and security of all those who believe in Him as Savior. How many will later be lost and perish? "I should lose nothing"! Can Jesus Christ lie or are His promises fully trustworthy because His sacrifice for our sins is finished forever?!

7. God has promised that you will *never perish, nor ever be snatched out of Christ's or the Father's hands*. (John 10:28-30)

Jesus Christ stated emphatically regarding His sheep (those who have believed in Him),

> And I give them *eternal life*, and they *shall never perish; neither shall anyone snatch them out of My hand*. My Father, who has given them to Me, is greater than all; and *no one is able to snatch them out of My Father's hand*. I and My Father are one. (John 10:28-30)

If you could somehow lose your salvation through sin, a lack of holiness, unfaithfulness, and so forth, then you would lose eternal life; you would perish; and you would somehow escape the hand of Jesus Christ and God the Father. Yet our Lord just guaranteed in absolute terms the impossibility of any of those circumstances occurring in your life. For, if you could do something to lose your salvation, then you would be required to do something to keep your salvation. If you must do something to keep your salvation, then your salvation would ultimately be determined by your works and faithfulness, instead of by Jesus Christ and His finished work on the cross. This would ultimately make salvation and going to Heaven a reward for your ongoing perseverance instead of being a gift of God's amazing grace. This is why the Bible contrasts grace and works (Romans 4:4-5; 11:6).

Dear believer, do not let anyone undermine the absolute assurance of your eternal salvation. This assurance is based upon the cross-work of Jesus Christ and the unfailing promises of God to the believer in Christ—not your faithfulness, holiness, religious works, or anything else to merit the favor of God (1 John 5:9-13). So be encouraged, dear believer, that you are accepted in Christ and saved and secure forever in God's love and grace regardless of what failures may come in your Christian life. Can you agree with Paul when he wrote,

> For I am persuaded that neither death nor life, nor angels nor principalities nor powers, nor things present nor things to come, nor height nor depth, nor any other created thing, shall be able to separate us from the love of God which is in Christ Jesus our Lord. (Rom. 8:38-39)

Let me ask you, do you stand persuaded and convinced of God's perpetual love for you and your eternal security based on the Scriptures? Do you have a hope-so temporal salvation or a know-so eternal salvation? God rendered His verdict in this courtroom scene of Romans 8:31-39, and it is clear: no one and nothing, at any time or place, whether angelic or human, can ever separate the born-again child of God from God's perpetual love. Now that is eternal security!

D. L. Moody, the gifted and down-to-earth evangelist of the nineteenth century, had an uncanny ability to personalize Scripture verses for needy hearts. J. Wilbur Chapman tells the following story of how Moody used John 5:24 to help him gain the assurance of his salvation.

> I was studying for the ministry, and I heard that D. L. Moody was to preach in Chicago. I went down to hear him. Finally I got into his after meeting. I shall never forget the thrill that went through me when he came and sat down beside me as an inquirer. He asked me if I was a Christian. I said, "Mr. Moody, I am not sure whether I am a Christian or not." He very kindly took his Bible and opened it at the fifth chapter of John, and the twenty-fourth verse, which reads as follows: "Verily, verily, I say unto you, he that heareth My word, and believeth on Him that sent Me, hath everlasting life, and shall not come into condemnation; but is passed from death unto life."
>
> "Suppose you had read it through for the first time, wouldn't you think it was wonderful?" I read it through, and he said, "Do you believe it?" I said, "Yes." "Do you accept it?" I said, "Yes." "Well, are you a Christian?" "Mr. Moody, I sometimes think I am, and sometimes I am afraid I am not." He very kindly said, "Read it again."
>
> So I read it again: "Verily, verily, I say unto you, he that heareth My word, and believeth on Him that sent me, hath everlasting life, and shall not come into condemnation; but is passed from death unto life." Then he said, "Do you believe it?" I said, "Yes." "Do you receive Him?" I said, "Yes." "Well," he said, "are you a Christian?" I just started to say over again that sometimes I was afraid I was not, when the only time in all the years I

knew him and loved him, he was sharp with me. He turned on me with his eyes flashing and said, "See here, whom you are doubting?" Then I saw it for the first time, that when I was afraid I was not a Christian I was doubting God's Word. I read it again with my eyes overflowing with tears.

Since that day I have had many sorrows and many joys, but never have I doubted for a moment that I was a Christian, because God said it.[1]

There are many more divine guarantees and scriptural reasons found throughout the Word of God that clearly indicate and teach that your salvation is eternal and secure in Christ. If you would like to read about these, permit me to recommend my book, *Shall Never Perish Forever*.[2]

---

[1]. "A Conversation between J. Wilbur Chapman and D. L. Moody," *Sword of the Lord* (October 28, 1988) as cited in Dennis Rokser, "Can You Know for Sure that You Are Eternally Saved and Secure? Part 2," *Grace Family Journal* 4 (May/June 2001): 27.
[2]. Dennis M. Rokser, *Shall Never Perish Forever: Is Salvation Forever or Can It Be Lost?* (Duluth, MN: Grace Gospel Press, 2012), 362 pp.

Your New Security

Chapter 6 Questions

Fill in the blanks and answer the following questions.

1. God declares that you are a _____.
   (John 1:12)

   a. Like your physical birth, what is true of your spiritual birth?

   b. What two scriptural concepts must you keep clear in your thinking?

   c. How often does entrance into the family of God occur?

   d. How often is fellowship with God to occur?

   e. What does sin in the life of the believer break?

   f. What does unconfessed sin in the life of the believer bring upon himself/herself?

   g. Does sin in the life of the child of God cause him/her to lose his/her salvation? Why?

h. Observe the chart on the Family of God and Fellowship with God and fill in the blanks below.

Once a person has placed his faith alone in _____ alone (John 1:12), he is forgiven of all sins and is placed in the _____ of God (Gal. 3:26). At the same time, the believer is also _____ by the Holy Spirit and becomes part of the body of Christ (1 Cor. 12:13). Although the believer will never be removed from the family of God, he must consistently confess his sins to remain in _____ with God (1 John 1:3-10).

2. God promises you that every believer in Christ _____ _____. (John 3:16)

   a. What verb tense is the word "have" in John 3:16?

   b. What does the word "have" mean?

   c. How long does "everlasting life" last?

   d. If this is true, can your new birth be undone later by sin in your Christian life, unfaithfulness, or carnality? Why?

3. God declares that either you _____ or else _____ it. (John 3:36)

   a. What is God's promise to the one who "believes in the Son"?

   b. What is God's two-fold evaluation about the one "who does not believe the Son"?

Your New Security

    c. What does this indicate about possessing everlasting life?

4. God has promised that you are guaranteed _____
_____. (John 5:24)

    a. According to John 5:24, what 3 things does God promise to give the person who believes God's Word?

    b. If a believer could lose his/her salvation through sin, unfaithfulness, carnality, or apostasy, how would these promises be contradicted by God (who cannot lie)?

5. God has promised that you will _____
_____. (John 6:35-37)

    a. What does Christ promise will never happen to the person who comes to Him by faith alone?

    b. If a believer could lose his salvation, how would these promises be contradicted by God (who cannot lie)?

    c. What can you conclude from these wonderful and unfailing promises of God that include the word "never"?

6. God has promised that in Christ you will _____ _____. (John 6:38-40)

   a. What is the three-fold promise of Jesus Christ to the believer in Him?

   b. If Jesus Christ will lose nothing, and the believer has everlasting life with the guarantee of a future bodily resurrection, what can you conclude from this?

7. God has promised that you will _____,
   nor ever be _____
   _____. (John 10:28-30)

   a. What are the four promises that Jesus Christ gives to those who "follow" (trust in) Him like a sheep with a shepherd?

   b. If a believer could lose his salvation through sin, a lack of holiness, unfaithfulness, etc., how would these promises be contradicted by God (who cannot lie)?

   c. If a believer could do something to lose his salvation, what would he be required to do?

Your New Security

d. If a believer was required to do something to stay saved or not lose eternal life, would salvation then depend on God or the believer?

e. If salvation was dependent upon the believer's walk, faithfulness, holiness, not sinning, ongoing confession of sin, perseverance, etc., would salvation be based upon God's grace or the believer's works?

f. How would this conclusion contradict Ephesians 2:8-9, and who then could the believer boast in?

g. If believers could somehow lose their salvation through sin, unfaithfulness, carnality, apostasy, etc., could they know for sure that they have eternal life and will go to Heaven when they die?

h. According to 1 John 5:13, what does God assure those who believe in the name of the Son of God?

i. According to Romans 8:38-39, what can every believer be persuaded of?

j. Is there any conditions or circumstances missing from God's perspective that could ever separate the believer from the love of God in Christ Jesus?

k. Are you persuaded that you are now and forever eternally secure in Christ?

Chapter 7

YOUR NEW PRIMARY MOTIVATION— THE LOVE OF CHRIST!

While the fear of eternal Hell is a great reason to be saved through faith in Christ alone, the fear of Hell is never given in Scripture as a reason now to live for Jesus Christ. Why? It is because the believer in Christ is saved and secure forever and no longer has any reason to fear Hell! Thus, what would motivate a believer now to serve Jesus Christ? The greatest motivators are the love of Christ, the work of Calvary, and the believer's new position or identification in Christ by God's grace.

> For *the love of Christ compels us*, because we judge thus: that *if One died for all*, then *all died*; and *He died for all*, that *those who live should live no longer for themselves, but for Him who died for them and rose again*. (2 Cor. 5:14-15)

It was Jesus Christ's love that compelled and motivated these believers now to live for Him. What a contrast to religion! God's love, not law, is to motivate the child of God to live a life that honors Jesus Christ. God's grace, not guilt or obligation, should compel the believer to live for Him who died for Him. How freeing and yet motivating to respond and rejoice in God's grace!

As you carefully reflect on God's love and grace from 2 Corinthians 5:14-15, you will notice that it always points you back to the great work of Christ at Calvary and the reality that the believer is now "in Christ" where God declares that believers "all died" with Him. This is how God views them—separated from their previous relationship to Adam as an unsaved, unregenerate person because they have died and are now related to Jesus Christ. But not only has every believer died with Christ, but the believer also lives with Christ ("those who live") with a new life as a result of their identity, union, or position in Jesus Christ. Thus, when you add up the facts ("because we thus judge"), the love of Jesus Christ, His death for all and resurrection, and their identification with Him, should motivate believers to "live no longer for themselves [which was true before salvation], but for Him who died for them and rose again."

The same motivating Christian-life truth can be observed in a nutshell from Galatians 2:20, which reads: "I have been crucified with Christ; it is no longer I who live, but Christ lives in me; and the life which I now live in the flesh I live by faith in the Son of God, who loved me and gave Himself for me" (Gal. 2:20). There is no greater motivator than that of love, especially the love of God toward us. Thus, "We love Him because He first loved us" (1 John 4:19). It is now reasonable for you to agree in your heart with the apostle Paul, who said in light of God's great salvation to him, "For to me, to live is Christ, and to die is gain" (Phil. 1:21).

The story has been told of a slave auction in New Orleans before the Proclamation of Emancipation in the USA. A beautiful black woman was to be sold to the highest bidder. The crowd was filled with lustful men who fantasized of their sexual immorality if this woman became their purchased possession, with many vocalizing it out loud with vulgarity. But it just so happened that a wealthy man of integrity and moral excellence wandered by the auction while all this was transpiring. At first he couldn't believe his ears and eyes as he observed these vile men expressing their lustful passions for this beautiful slave and their desire to purchase her. And he found himself moved with compassion for her and a desire to rescue her from her degrading future. So he entered the bidding, which quickly escalated to a large sum of money until he saw the auctioneer point in his direction and yell out, "Sold!" He had purchased this woman at great personal expense. He then went to claim his purchased slave only for her to

Your New Primary Motivation

spit in his face and curse, "I hate you," as she anticipated that his purchase of her was generated by similar motives as the other men. What would happen in the next couple minutes would be shocking to her and all who were privy to it. This kind, gracious man turned to her and said, "I purchased you out of love and compassion to rescue you from these other men. Now I am setting you free." In utter dismay and unbelief the woman replied, "What did you say?" Again the man explained, "I bought you because I cared for your soul. But I have no intentions of misusing or abusing you. I am setting you free." This female slave, overwhelmed by the grace shown to her and the great sum the man had paid to purchase her exclaimed, "No one has ever loved me like this. I want to serve you all the days of my life." Dear believer, do you see the spiritual analogy? God's great grace and sacrificial love toward us should produce a love for Christ in which we now joyfully serve Him, not because we have to, but because we want to.

Chapter 7 Questions

1. What is NOT a scriptural reason to serve the Lord after a sinner has been saved? Why?

2. What are three great motivators now to live for Jesus Christ once a person is saved?

3. Can you identify these three great motivations to live for Christ in 2 Corinthians 5:14-15?

4. Instead of being motivated by God's law, what should now motivate the believer in Christ?

5. Instead of being motivated by guilt or obligation, what should now motivate the believer in Christ?

6. How does God now view the believer in light of the death and resurrection of Jesus Christ and your identity / position in Him?

Your New Primary Motivation

7. Can you state two more passages of Scripture that support the love of Christ as a key motivator now to walk with Him and love Him?

8. Complete this verse: "For to me to live is _____, and to die is _____." (Phil. 1:21)

9. What does the illustration of the slave auction in New Orleans years ago set forth?

10. Have you decided to live for Jesus Christ who died for you and rose again?

11. Why don't believers in Christ choose to live daily for Jesus Christ?

12. What are some other valid, biblical motivations to live for the Lord as a believer?

Chapter 8

YOUR NEW PERSPECTIVE OF PEOPLE—
IN ADAM OR IN CHRIST!

As the Word of God is now allowed to impact your thinking and perspectives in life, it will not only change how you view God and yourself but it will cause you to look at people from a divine perspective instead of a human viewpoint.

> Therefore, from now on, we regard no one according to the flesh. Even though we have known Christ according to the flesh, yet now we know Him thus no longer. Therefore, if anyone is in Christ, he is a new creation; old things have passed away; behold, all things have become new. (2 Cor. 5:16-17)

Your new perspective will cause you to no longer regard people "according to the flesh" or based upon human standards. While still recognizing distinct differences among people, the bottom-line issue in your thinking will no longer be their race, gender, language, ethnicity, and so on. Instead it will be whether they are still "in Adam" (identified with the first man as part of his family) or now "in Christ" (as identified with Him as part of God's family). It will be whether they are saved or lost, whether they are on their way to Heaven or still on their way to Hell, and whether they are a child of God or a child of the Devil. What makes the difference? Their response to Jesus Christ as presented in the Gospel of grace! Shouldn't this now make us deeply concerned that sinners become saved by God's grace before it's too late?!

Some years ago in England a condemned assassin, Charles Peace, was being led to the scaffold to die. At his side walked a pastor who began speaking to him of the finished work of Christ. After some time, Charles Peace suddenly demanded, "Do you really believe what you have just been telling me?" "Certainly, I do," replied the pastor, a bit shaken by the vehemence of the question. "No, you don't," declared Peace with a hard tone. "If I believed what you say you believe, I would crawl across England on my hands and knees over fields strewn with broken glass to tell men and women about it. You don't believe it yourself!"

May we live out practically what we believe is true from the Word of God and thus view people differently than we did before we became new creations in Christ. And may we increasingly let God use us to impact others for Jesus Christ in the sphere of influence that He has given us.

Chapter 8 Questions

1. As a result of becoming a new creation in Christ, God wants to transform the thinking of believers through His Word so that they no longer view other people from what perspective?

2. How does God want believers now to view others?

3. As believers view people from a new creation perspective, what questions will they now take into consideration?

4. How should these truths move us practically toward the unsaved?

Chapter 9

YOUR NEW MINISTRY AND PRIVILEGE—
AN AMBASSADOR FOR JESUS CHRIST!

When you became a new creation in Christ, why didn't God immediately take you home to Heaven? Why did He leave you on this planet? One important reason is because God has given you a new ministry and privilege as an ambassador for Jesus Christ.

> Now all things are of God, who has reconciled us to Himself through Jesus Christ, and has given us the ministry of reconciliation, that is, that God was in Christ reconciling the world to Himself, not imputing their trespasses to them, and has committed to us the word of reconciliation. Now then, we are ambassadors for Christ, as though God were pleading through us: we implore you on Christ's behalf, be reconciled to God. (2 Cor. 5:18-20)

God wants all sinners to be saved and to come to the knowledge of the truth of the Gospel (1 Tim. 2:4) before it's too late. He wants to reconcile sinners to Himself through Jesus Christ and His ransom payment at Calvary (1 Tim. 2:5-6). To accomplish this reconciliation which He made available to all through "the blood of His cross" (Col. 1:20), God now seeks to use saved sinners as His heralds of the message of reconciliation so that others may hear and believe. Thus, God wants to mature you and

Your New Ministry and Privilege

use you as an "ambassador for Christ." An ambassador acts as a representative of the head of another country, living on foreign turf, and faithfully communicating the message of His King to the inhabitants of the land. In a similar fashion, believers are Christ's ambassadors. Although our new home is in Heaven (John 14:1-3; Phil. 3:20-21), we are left here on earth to proclaim the Gospel of salvation to the lost around us. Aren't you glad that someone presented the Gospel to you! And to think that you now have a purpose in life bigger than yourself and that God wants to use you by His grace to share the Gospel with others!

While you may be both untrained and even fearful of sharing the Gospel with others (this is very normal, especially for newer believers), you can begin right now to pray for the salvation of others, perhaps give them a piece of sound evangelistic material (like the *John 3:16 Illustrated* booklet), and begin to learn how to share the good news of the Gospel with others (perhaps by watching others explain John 3:16[1]). God will faithfully bring you along by His grace to gain a greater understanding and confidence in explaining the Gospel to others. Just be willing to let the Lord equip, mature, and use you by His grace. He can and will!

There is no greater message than the Gospel of grace, which proclaims the great exchange—our sin given to Christ and His righteousness given to us by simple faith in Him alone: "For He made Him who knew no sin to be sin for us, that we might become the righteousness of God in Him" (2 Cor. 5:21).

But keep in mind that life is short, eternity is long, and death is certain. We must redeem the time with a pilgrim mentality as ambassadors for Christ and capture the opportunities He gives us to serve Him and make the Gospel known. Then one day, we'll be going home to Heaven where we now belong.

This is like the missionary who faithfully served and suffered for Jesus Christ in Africa for preaching the Gospel, teaching the Word of God, and planting churches amidst much opposition. After a few years he and his wife were finally coming back to the United States to enjoy a year of furlough. After they sailed on a crowded ship to New York harbor, they were surprised to see a

---

1. To view a video explanation of "The John 3:16 Fair Diagram Explained," see the link given at the bottom of page 6.

band and many dignitaries awaiting the arrival of the ship. Unbeknown to them there was on their ship a very famous American president, Teddy Roosevelt, who was returning from a safari on the Zambezi River by Livingstone, Zambia. The crowds had come to greet the president and had dispersed by the time this godly couple had been able to depart the ship. The devoted missionary turned to his wife with disappointment in his voice, "There is no one here to greet us." His wise wife, with divine viewpoint flooding her mind, aptly replied, "Honey, we need to remember that we are not really home yet."

Chapter 9 Questions

1. When you were saved by God's grace through faith alone in Christ alone, what was a major reason God did not take you home immediately to Heaven?

2. Does God want all sinners to be saved and to come to the knowledge of the truth of the Gospel?

3. For God to accomplish the reconciliation of sinners to Himself based on the finished work of Jesus Christ, what does God now want to do with saved sinners?

4. What spiritual truth is pictured by the metaphor of believers being "ambassadors" for Jesus Christ?

5. What does the truth of being an "ambassador for Christ" mean to you personally?

6. While you may be untrained in evangelism and afraid to witness for Christ, what are some things that you can do right now?

7. What is another extremely helpful resource to watch and learn how to present the Gospel to others?

8. Can you explain the "great exchange" according to 2 Corinthians 5:21?

9. Since our time on earth is short and eternity is long, what should believers seek to do?

10. If you are in a group, go around the group and take some time to discuss your burdens for the lost you know, writing down their names and praying for them.

Chapter 10

YOUR NEW MEANS OF COMMUNICATION WITH GOD— THE WORD OF GOD & BELIEVING PRAYER!

As a new believer in Jesus Christ it is vital that you remember that true biblical Christianity is not a religion of human achievement but a relationship with God of divine accomplishment. As a result of being born again, God now wants the believer to grow spiritually, to learn to walk by faith, and to enjoy a sweet fellowship with the Lord each day. But how does a born-again child of God now grow? "As newborn babes, desire the pure milk of the word, that you may grow thereby"(1 Peter 2:2). Just as a newborn baby has a great longing for his mother's milk, so believers are to intensely choose to desire the milk of God's Word to grow spiritually. This is also encouraged by the new nature you received at your new birth which has desires for the Word of God.

This is why purchasing a good study Bible can be very helpful. (I recommend the Scofield Study Bible, New King James Version.) This is also where finding, if possible, a good Bible-believing church in your area can also be extremely beneficial. But let me caution you regarding this. Many churches give lip service to the Bible but do not clearly preach the Gospel or teach the Bible verse by verse. Furthermore, many deny the wonderful truths of grace which you have read about in this book—the eternal security of the believer, your identity or position in Christ, and other biblical truths. Pray for wisdom and God's leading in this matter. Also, do not hesitate to access the thousands of online

Bible studies on various books and subjects of the Bible at our website.[1]

God speaks to you today not in visions, dreams, or ecstatic experiences, but through the reading, study, and memorization of His Word. Thus, Jesus Christ stated emphatically,

> It is written, "Man shall not live by bread alone, but by every word that proceeds from the mouth of God." (Matt. 4:4)

In addition, God will use His Word to transform you internally to become more and more like Jesus Christ.

> But we all, with unveiled face, beholding as in a mirror the glory of the Lord, are being transformed into the same image from glory to glory, just as by the Spirit of the Lord. (2 Cor. 3:18)

Furthermore, God desires to use His Word to cleanse your way, keep you from sin, and direct your life path.

> How can a young man cleanse his way? By taking heed according to Your word. With my whole heart I have sought You; Oh, let me not wander from Your commandments! Your word I have hidden in my heart, that I might not sin against You! (Ps. 119:9-11)

> Your word is a lamp to my feet and a light to my path. (Ps. 119:105)

The Word of God is vital to your spiritual growth; but your fellowship with the Lord doesn't stop there. Just as a dialogue is preferable to a monologue in any relationship, so God has given His children the privilege to pray to Him in praise, thanksgiving, admission or confession of sin (for fellowship with God), and making requests for others and for our own needs. Consider the following verses that relate to various aspects of prayer:

---

1. See www.duluthbible.org/sermons

> Be anxious for nothing, but in everything by prayer and supplication, with thanksgiving, let your requests be made known to God; and the peace of God, which surpasses all understanding, will guard your hearts and minds through Christ Jesus. (Phil. 4:6-7)

> If we confess our sins, He is faithful and just to forgive us our sins and to cleanse us from all unrighteousness. (1 John 1:9)

> Ask, and it will be given to you; seek, and you will find; knock, and it will be opened to you. For everyone who asks receives, and he who seeks finds, and to him who knocks it will be opened. (Matt. 7:7-8)

> The effective, fervent prayer of a righteous man avails much. (James 5:16)

You may be wondering, "If God is all-knowing and in control, why even pray?" It is important to remember that while God is sovereign, yet He amazingly factors our prayers into His plans and will for us. Thus, we should ask the Lord in faith to consider our petitions and to act according to His will.

> If any of you lacks wisdom, let him ask of God, who gives to all liberally and without reproach, and it will be given to him. But let him ask in faith, with no doubting, for he who doubts is like a wave of the sea driven and tossed by the wind. (James 1:5-6)

> Now this is the confidence that we have in Him, that if we ask anything according to His will, He hears us. And if we know that He hears us, whatever we ask, we know that we have the petitions that we have asked of Him. (1 John 5:14-15)

CHRISTIAN LIFE BY GRACE

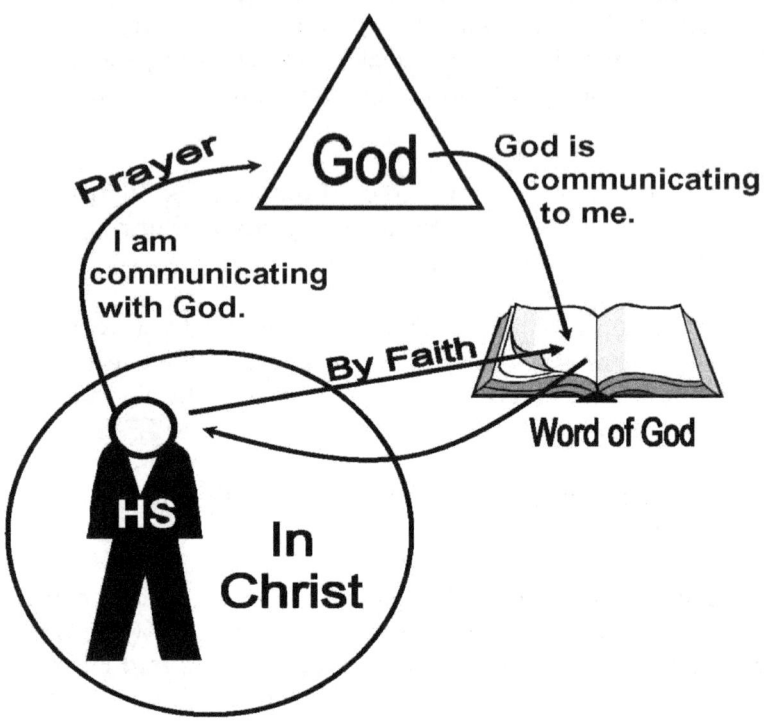

What an amazing realization that the God of the universe is your Heavenly Father now that you've been born again, and that you can talk directly to Him in prayer about whatever is on your heart because of Jesus Christ ("in Jesus' Name")! There is no special language needed for you to pray. God knows your words and heart and He desires your fellowship. It might be helpful to keep in mind that the elements of prayer can be divided into three aspects (using a golfing term or acrostic):

P – Praise to God for His many spiritual and physical blessings in your life by His grace because of Jesus Christ

A – Admission of your sins when they occur and as needed

R – Requests for the needs of others as well as yourself

Your New Means of Communication with God

Like everything in the Christian life, if you are willing God will use His Word to mature you by His grace when it comes to learning how to pray effectively, just like your communication skills increased as you grew from childhood to adulthood.

Chapter 10 Questions

1. Is true Christianity a "religion"?

2. As a result of being born again, what are three spiritual realities that God wants to occur in your life as a believer?

3. How does the analogy of a new-born baby relate to your spiritual growth as a believer? (1 Peter 2:2)

4. In light of the believer's need to learn sound, biblical teaching, what are some recommendations?

5. How does God speak to you today?

6. Fill in the blanks: Jesus Christ said, "Man shall not live on bread _____, but by every _____ that proceeds from the _____." (Matthew 4:4)

Your New Means of Communication with God

7. Being likened to a mirror, what does God use to transform believers internally by the Holy Spirit?

8. According to Psalm 119:9-11, how does God want to use His Word in the believer's life?

9. According to Psalm 119:105, what is another benefit of learning the Word of God?

10. Does God ideally want a monologue or a dialogue with His children? How is this possible?

11. What are four elements to include in your prayer to God?

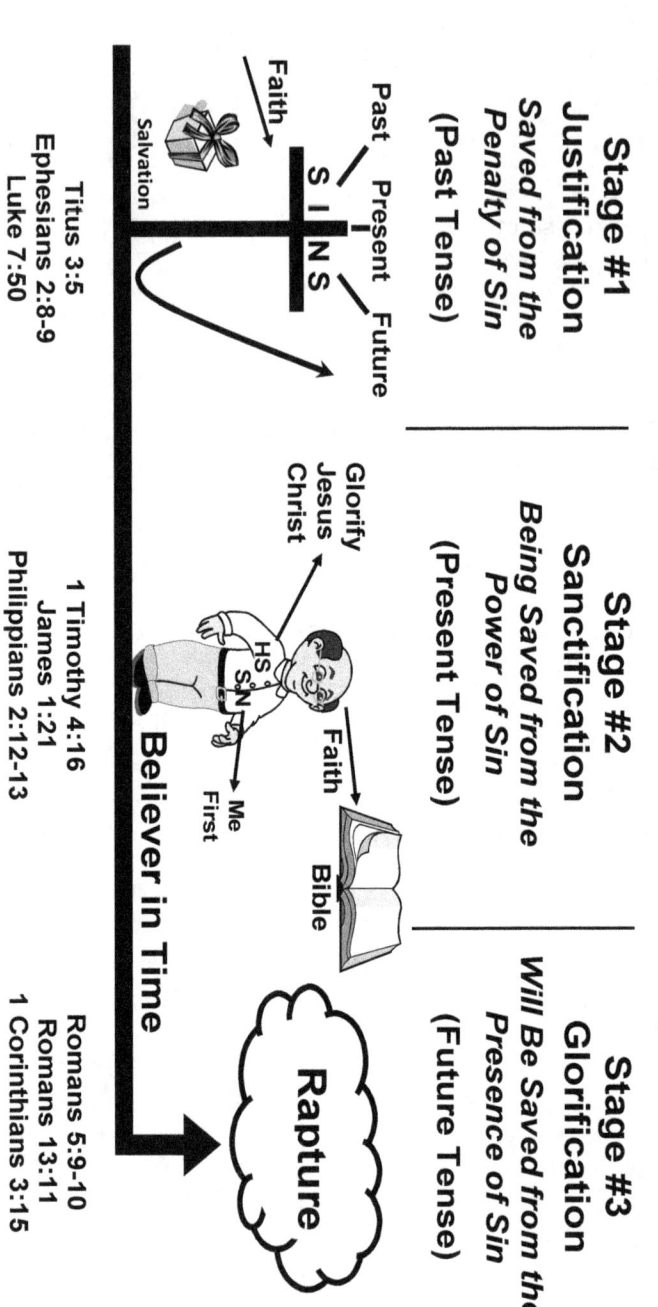

Chapter 11

YOUR NEW UNDERSTANDING OF GOD'S PLAN FOR YOU—THE THREE TENSES OF SALVATION!

One of the most important foundational truths that you must firmly grasp from God's Word is the three tenses, phases, or stages of God's plan of spiritual salvation for you. I would encourage you to study carefully the chart on the previous page that outlines this vital truth of the Scriptures. Clarity regarding this biblical concept will eliminate much confusion that will otherwise fog your thinking when reading the Scriptures.

At the moment you placed your faith in Jesus Christ and what He did for you on the cross, you were instantaneously saved from the *penalty of sin*, which is eternal death or Hell. You can now confidently speak of your salvation in the past tense:

> Not by works of righteousness which we have done, but according to His mercy *He saved us*. (Titus 3:5)

> For by grace *you have been saved* through faith, and that not of yourselves; it is the gift of God. (Eph. 2:8)

This stage of your salvation is completed in the past, never to be reversed, and is absolutely guaranteed because it depends solely upon Christ's work for you on the cross.

Upon having trusted in Jesus Christ, you have now entered the second phase or stage of God's plan of salvation which involves God now wanting to save you daily from the *power of sin* in your Christian life. Though you are a new creation in Christ, you still retain inside of you a sinful nature that wants to rule your life in opposition to God (Rom. 6:12). This old sin nature manifested itself in your past with certain patterns of sin or addictions that kept you in practical bondage such as pride, bitterness, drunkenness, sexual immorality, and so forth. God now wants you to know that the sin nature has been stripped of it's authority to rule in your life as king since you are in Christ and He is your Lord (Rom. 6:1-11).

Salvation or deliverance from sin's power also involves God replacing our human viewpoint and worldly thinking with His divine viewpoint through the Word of God (Rom. 12:2). In addition, though Satan was unable to stop you from trusting in Jesus Christ as your Savior, he now wants to hinder you from walking and growing in the Lord through persecution or worldly distraction so that you will not become fruitful for Jesus Christ and impact others for the Savior (Luke 8:13-15). But none of these obstacles has taken the Lord by surprise and He has provided everything necessary for you to live a life of godliness and victory over sin out of gratitude for your Savior (2 Peter 1:2-4).

Thus, God has already saved you from *sin's penalty* and He now wants to save you daily from *sin's power* while you await the day that you will be saved forever from *sin's presence* in Heaven. This is why Paul wrote to the Christians in Rome to remind them: "And do this, knowing the time, that now it is high time to awake out of sleep; *for now our salvation is nearer than when we first believed*" (Rom. 13:11).

Since these Roman Christians had already believed in Christ as their Savior, they were saved forever from sin's *penalty*; but they were now to live with spiritual alertness (rather than spiritual sleepiness) because each advancing day brought them nearer to their future salvation from sin's very *presence*. Notice, also, that this future salvation was absolutely certain for these believers. They knew they were saved from Hell and eternally secure; but now they were being encouraged to live in light of this future reality. If they would do so, they would experience salvation from sin's power in their lives and not waste the opportunity to live for the Lord Jesus Christ in the meantime.[1]

---

1. For further explanation of the three tenses of salvation, see Dennis M. Rokser, *Salvation in Three Time Zones* (Duluth, MN: Grace Gospel Press, 2013).

Your New Understanding of God's Plan for You!

Chapter 11 Questions

1. How many phases, stages, or tenses are involved in God's plan of salvation? (Study the chart at the beginning of the chapter.)

2. What aspect of sin were you saved from the moment you placed your faith in Christ as Savior?

3. Fill in the blanks: For by _____ you _____ saved through _____, and that not of yourselves; it is the _____ of God. (Ephesians 2:8-9)

4. What aspect of sin does God now want to save / deliver you from daily?

5. Why is this "salvation" needed in your daily Christian life?

6. What does God now want you to know regarding the sin nature's right to rule in your life?

7. Why else is salvation from sin's power needed in our lives?

8. What are two ways that Satan seeks to hinder your spiritual growth in Christ?

9. What aspect of deliverance from sin does the third phase or stage of God's plan of salvation for you involve?

10. Is this phase of salvation guaranteed and where will it ultimately be experienced?

11. Can you remember the 3 phases or tenses of salvation for the believer in Christ?

Chapter 12

YOUR NEW OPPORTUNITY—TO GROW SPIRITUALLY!

While spiritual birth must precede spiritual growth, God now wants you to grow in grace and become more and more like His Son, Jesus Christ. This is what progressive sanctification and spiritual growth is all about.

> *Having been born again,* not of corruptible seed but incorruptible, *through the word of God* which lives and abides forever, because "All flesh is as grass, and all the glory of man as the flower of the grass. The grass withers, and its flower falls away, but the word of the LORD endures forever." Now *this is the word which by the gospel was preached to you.* Therefore, laying aside all malice, all deceit, hypocrisy, envy, and all evil speaking, *as newborn babes, desire the pure milk of the word, that you may grow thereby,* if indeed you have tasted that the Lord is gracious. (1 Peter 1:23—2:3)

Spiritual birth should result in spiritual growth as the believer progresses from Christian babyhood, to spiritual adolescence, to becoming a mature believer in the faith (1 John 2:13-14). Since you have already tasted that the Lord is gracious when you believed the Gospel and were born again, why not desire now the pure milk of the Word in order to grow by further tasting and understanding God's amazing grace? While there is nothing wrong with being a babe in Christ (since we all begin there!), there is definitely something wrong if you remain a babe in your growth (1 Cor. 3:1-2) or later retrogress back into spiritual immaturity after you have grown in your knowledge of God's Word and in personal faith, hope, and love (Heb. 5:11-12).

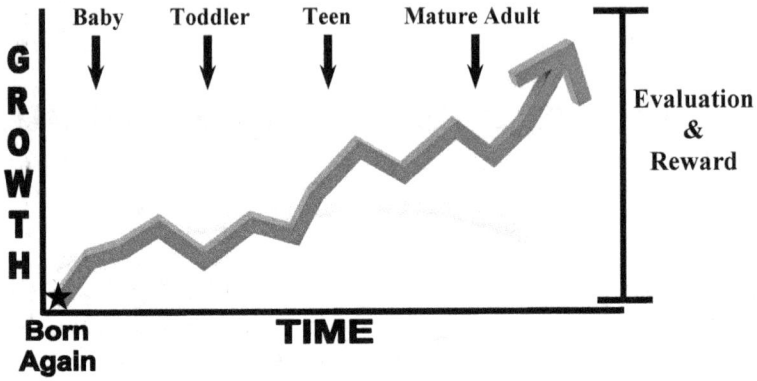

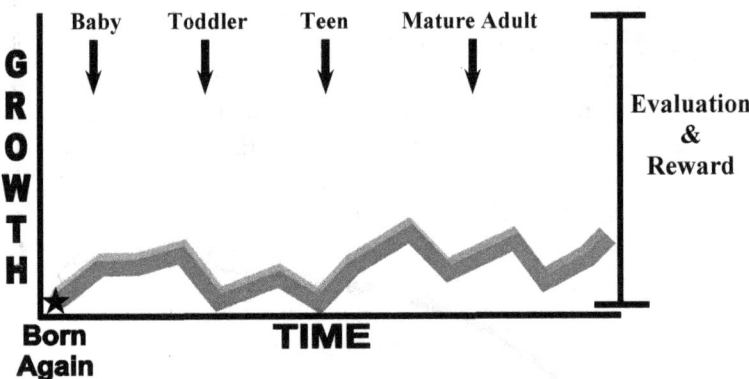

But this raises an important question, namely, how does a believer grow spiritually? Like with your salvation from sin's penalty, God has provided everything necessary by His grace for you to grow as a child of God, except for the faith that you must learn to exercise in daily dependence upon Him and His promises. So, what is involved in God's grace-design for your spiritual growth?

1. Spiritual growth takes TIME. (Hebrews 5:12)
While spiritual birth happens at a moment of time, spiritual maturity does not occur overnight; it takes time. *"For though by this time* you ought to be teachers, you need someone to teach you again the first principles of the oracles of God; and you have come to need milk and not solid food" (Heb. 5:12).

We need to be patient when it comes to our spiritual growth. God is not in a hurry and it takes time to grow. Think of the little baby. This baby doesn't even think about growing and certainly isn't in a hurry. As the baby simply takes in proper food, and allows the parents to care for him, his growth happens automatically. The same should be true of us as believers. We need to simply enjoy the Lord, feed on His Word, and growth will occur over time, many times without us even realizing it. Remember that when God wants to produce a squash, He takes six months. But when God wants to produce a solid oak tree, He takes a hundred years. Which one do you want to be? This is important to remember because there are many adjustments God wants to make in your thinking, motives, and relationships; but He does so graciously and patiently, in love, over time.

2. Spiritual growth takes TRUTH. (Hebrews 5:12-13)
"For though by this time you ought to be teachers, *you need someone to teach you again the first principles of the oracles of God; and you have come to need milk* and not solid food. For everyone who partakes only of milk is unskilled in the word of righteousness, for he is a babe." (Heb. 5:12-13)

The great need of your Christian life is not to do "great things for God." Instead it is to get firmly established in the Word of God through the personal reading and public teaching of the Scriptures.

> Study to show thyself approved unto God, a workman that needs not to be ashamed, rightly dividing the word of truth. (2 Tim. 2:15, KJV)

> All Scripture is given by inspiration of God, and is profitable for doctrine, for reproof, for correction, for instruction in righteousness, that the man of God may be complete [mature], thoroughly equipped for every good work. (2 Tim. 3:16-17)

If you are going to grow spiritually, the regular intake of the milk and meat of the Word of God is essential.

3. Spiritual growth requires sound TEACHERS.
For though by this time you ought to be teachers, *you need someone to teach you again the first principles of the oracles of God*; and you have come to need milk and not solid food. (Heb. 5:12-13)

In order to facilitate your spiritual growth through a correct understanding of the Scriptures, God has given to you *the Holy Spirit* as your inner and ultimate teacher. "Now we have received, not the spirit of the world, but the Spirit who is from God, that we might know the things that have been freely given to us by God" (1 Cor. 2:12).

It is through the teaching ministry of the Holy Spirit that the believer can understand God's Word. The Lord wants you to know the truth and He is willing to personally teach you through His Spirit who indwells you. So before you begin to read the Scriptures, pray for spiritual understanding and enlightenment like the Psalmist who uttered, "Open my eyes, that I may see wondrous things from Your law" (Ps. 119:18).

In addition, God has also provided *human teachers* as grace-gifts to the Church.

> And He Himself gave some to be apostles, some prophets, some evangelists, and some pastors and teachers, for the equipping of the saints for the work of ministry, for the edifying of the body of Christ, till we all come to the unity of the faith and of the knowledge of the Son of God, to a perfect man, to the measure of the stature of the fullness of Christ; that we should no longer be children, tossed to and fro and carried about with every wind of doctrine,

> by the trickery of men, in the cunning craftiness of deceitful plotting, but, [by] speaking the truth in love, may grow up in all things into Him who is the head—Christ. (Eph. 4:11-15)

Though apostles and prophets were only needed to act as a foundation for the early church and have since passed off the scene (Eph. 2:20), God still uses "evangelists" to preach the Gospel, plant churches, and train others to do so, along with using "pastors and teachers" to spiritually equip believers with sound doctrine. Unfortunately, there is a lot of false teaching in churches today so that the Gospel is not preached in its clarity and verse-by-verse exposition of the Scriptures has been replaced with an emphasis on musical performances and entertainment. The apostle Paul explained the need for biblical preaching and the anticipated replacement of sound teaching in churches when he wrote,

> Preach the word! Be ready in season and out of season. Convince, rebuke, exhort, with all longsuffering and teaching. For the time will come when they will not endure sound doctrine, but according to their own desires, because they have itching ears, they will heap up for themselves teachers; and they will turn their ears away from the truth, and be turned aside to fables. (2 Tim. 4:2-4)

These verses emphasize the importance of hearing the preaching and teaching of the Word of God. However, this passage also prophetically predicts what we see happening in many churches today, namely, giving ear-tickling sermons based on what people want and what will stroke their flesh rather than preaching the Word of God which will meet people's real spiritual needs. It stands to reason that if a church cannot present the Gospel to you clearly enough so that you can be saved, it will not provide you with the sound biblical doctrine you need to grow. So always begin by finding out what a church believes about the Gospel and how to be saved.

Though I highly recommend that you be a part of a local church where the Gospel of grace is clearly preached and where the Bible is clearly taught, such churches are also increasingly becoming few and far between. A good place to begin your search for a sound local church would be to contact the person, or attend the local church, that gave you this booklet. If this isn't possible, you are always welcome and invited to watch a live webcast or download various studies from God's Word from our church's website (www.duluthbible.org), or contact us at the phone number listed at the back of this book. But if you do find a sound Bible-teaching church in your area, be sure to take to heart the following encouragement: "And let us consider one another in order to stir up love and good works, *not forsaking the assembling of ourselves together, as is the manner of some*, but exhorting one another, and so much the more as you see the Day approaching" (Heb. 10:24-25).

Furthermore, spiritual instruction and encouragement from other believers that are farther along in their understanding of the Word of God will prove to be very beneficial in your own spiritual growth. But let me caution you to always compare and confirm everything that is taught with the Word of God to discern whether it lines up with the Scriptures (Acts 17:10-12).

4. Spiritual growth requires TRIALS. (James 1:2-4)

"For though by this time you ought to be teachers, you need someone to teach you again the first principles of the oracles of God; and you have come to need milk and not solid food. For everyone who partakes only of milk is *unskilled in the word of righteousness*, for he is a babe." (Heb. 5:12-13)

The word "unskilled" in verse 13 literally means "without experience" or "no trial." It could be used of someone who audits a class, meaning that they simply sit through the class but aren't required to take any tests. Tests do something very important for a student. They force the student to study and know the material if they want to pass the test. As a teacher, if you never gave any tests, guess what your students would do. NOTHING! In the same way, God provides "tests" for believers to give us opportunities to apply His word. Without these tests, we would fall asleep and not see the need for Him and His Word.

> My brethren, count it all joy when you fall into various trials, knowing that the testing of your faith produces patience. But let patience have its perfect work, that you may be perfect and complete, lacking nothing. (Jam. 1:2-4)

Why does God allow trials in your life? He is testing your faith and seeking to produce "patience" in your life (v. 3). It is only when you "know" this (v. 3) that you can accept by faith God's purpose for your trials and therefore "count it all joy." Why does God allow trials in your life? It is for the purpose of you becoming "perfect and complete" or spiritually balanced and mature (v. 4). God is more interested in your spiritual growth than He is in your personal comfort. Now some people think that difficulties and trials are a sign of God's displeasure in their lives. Yes, some trials and suffering are self-induced because of bad choices we have made (Gal. 6:7-8). Other trials and suffering are simply the result of the fact that we live in a physical body that is under the curse of disease and death stemming from Adam's sin (Rom. 5:12; 8:17-25). But many trials that believers face are designed to get our attention and teach us to trust the Lord and His promises instead of relying on our own wisdom and strength. This refining of your faith is invaluable to your spiritual maturation.

> Blessed be the God and Father of our Lord Jesus Christ, who according to His abundant mercy has begotten us again to a living hope through the resurrection of Jesus Christ from the dead, to an inheritance incorruptible and undefiled and that does not fade away, reserved in heaven for you, who are kept by the power of God through faith for salvation ready to be revealed in the last time. In this you greatly rejoice, though now for a little while, if need be, you have been grieved by various trials, that the genuineness of your faith, being much more precious than gold that perishes, though it is tested by fire, may be found to praise, honor, and glory at the revelation of Jesus Christ. (1 Peter 1:3-7)

God allows trials in your life to keep you dependent on Him and growing in grace in order to make you more like His Son. This reminds me of a story about codfish, where, in the northeastern United States, these fish are not only delectable but are a big commercial business. At one point, the supply of such fish could not keep pace with the demand, especially the demand for fresh cod. At first, suppliers would freeze the fish and ship them to various places, but the freezing process took away much of the flavor. So they experimented with shipping the fish alive in tanks of seawater, but this proved to be even worse since it was not only very expensive but by the time the cod arrived, they were soft and mushy. Finally, one creative person solved the problem with an innovative idea. The codfish were placed into a tank of water along with their natural enemy—the catfish. From the time the cod left the East Coast until they arrived at their western destinations, the catfish chased the cod all over the tank so that the cod were as fresh as they were when they were first caught! There was no loss of flavor and their texture was not adversely affected. If anything, the cod were better than before.

Could it be that God has allowed a catfish in your tank to keep you turning in faith to the Lord and growing spiritually, instead of getting soft, mushy, and flavorless? Can you name the catfish in your tank? Perhaps you live with one of them? Or is it someone you work with whose irritating presence drives you to your knees every day? Isn't it time to stop the griping, complaining, and pity-party, and start thanking God for the catfish in your tank and how "all things are working together for good" (Rom. 8:28) in your life? Yes, you may ask the Lord to remove your "thorn in the flesh"—Paul did three times (2 Cor. 12:7-8). But be prepared for the Lord to say in essence to you, "My grace is sufficient for you. My strength is made perfect in weakness." Someone has said that a Christian is like a teabag; he's not of much use until he's been through some hot water.

5. Spiritual growth requires TRUST. (Hebrews 11:6)
But without faith it is impossible to please Him, for he who comes to God must believe that He is, and that He is a rewarder of those who diligently seek Him. (Heb. 11:6)

Your New Opportunity

Faith is the only response that pleases God. Any other response involves human wisdom or human good, and those emanate from the flesh and do not give God the glory. The men and women in the Bible who pleased God over the centuries (several are mentioned in Hebrews 11) did so because they trusted in the Lord and His Word. In contrast, those who did not please the Lord did not respond by faith in God's provisions or promises. They made the foolish mistake of thinking, "I can handle it."

> Therefore, since a promise remains of entering His rest, let us fear lest any of you seem to have come short of it. For indeed the gospel was preached to us as well as to them; *but the word which they heard did not profit them, not being mixed with faith in those who heard it.* (Heb. 4:1-2)

Notice that the message of God's rest for us as believers does not profit us unless it is mixed with faith. Like water must be mixed with cement to form concrete, so your willingness to trust daily in God's unfailing person, principles, or promises is needed to enter the spiritual rest that God makes available to you in your Christian life. You can hear God's Word, memorize God's Word, and know God's Word to the point of being a walking, talking Bible encyclopedia, but it won't profit you personally unless you believe God's promises. The past Exodus generation of Jews did not please God because of their unbelief, but He still offers His daily faith-rest life to you and me today.

> There remains therefore a rest for the people of God. For he who has entered His rest has himself also ceased from his works as God did from His. Let us therefore be diligent to enter that rest, lest anyone fall according to the same example of disobedience. (Heb. 4:9-11)

How does a person enter into this spiritual rest of inner tranquility and peace that God desires His people to enjoy daily? It is by believing God's Word and resting by faith in His promises to us amidst the trials and tribulations of life. We must cease from our works and efforts in trying to help God out (v. 10) and rest daily by faith in God's plan and promises to us.

We can only apply God's Word when we believe His Word. If we want to grow, we need to respond to God's Word by faith, and through His Spirit apply the truth in our lives. The "unskilled" believer of Hebrews 5:13 is contrasted with the believer who "by reason of use" (5:14) has applied the truth and has received some spiritual "exercise." And according to verse 14, an evidence of spiritual growth is that the believer can "discern both good and evil" and therefore not be "tossed to and fro" with false doctrine.

Consider the following promises from God that you can learn and believe each day in the trials and decisions of life.

> Blessed be the God and Father of our Lord Jesus Christ, the Father of mercies and God of all comfort, who comforts us in all our tribulation, that we may be able to comfort those who are in any trouble, with the comfort with which we ourselves are comforted by God. (2 Cor. 1:3-4)

> No temptation has overtaken you except such as is common to man; but God is faithful, who will not allow you to be tempted beyond what you are able, but with the temptation will also make the way of escape, that you may be able to bear it. (1 Cor. 10:13)

> And we know that all things work together for good to those who love God, to those who are the called according to His purpose. For whom He foreknew, He also predestined to be conformed to the image of His Son, that He might be the firstborn among many brethren. (Rom. 8:28-29)

> If we are faithless, He remains faithful; He cannot deny Himself. (2 Tim. 2:13)

> But He knows the way that I take; when He has tested me, I shall come forth as gold. (Job 23:10)

> You will keep him in perfect peace, whose mind is stayed on You, because he trusts in You. Trust in the LORD forever, for in YAH, the LORD, is everlasting strength. (Isa. 26:3-4)

> Trust in the LORD with all your heart, and lean not on your own understanding; in all your ways acknowledge Him, and He shall direct your paths. (Prov. 3:5-6)

If you would like a more complete listing of God's promises, let me encourage you to read the booklet, *The Promises of God for the Child of God*.[1]

So how do you grow spiritually? Spiritual growth requires TIME, TRUTH, TEACHERS, TRIALS, and TRUST. Are you willing to let God bring you through the process of spiritual growth stage-by-stage to make you more and more like His Son? You will be glad you did!

> But we all, with unveiled face, beholding as in a mirror the glory of the Lord, are being transformed into the same image from glory to glory, just as by the Spirit of the Lord. (2 Cor. 3:18)

> Now may the God of hope fill you with all joy and peace in believing, that you may abound in hope by the power of the Holy Spirit. (Rom. 15:13)

> So then faith comes by hearing, and hearing by the Word of God. (Rom. 10:17)

I would love to expand further on some key truths of your position/identity in Christ and how to faith-rest in Christ as your Life through the power of the Holy Spirit (Romans 6–8), but space does not permit me to do so here. But when you have finished this short book, I would encourage you to read next the booklet, *I'm Saved but Struggling with Sin! Is Victory Available?*[2]

---

1. www.duluthbible.org/gracegospelpress/booklets/booklets-listing
2. www.duluthbible.org/gracegospelpress/booklets

Chapter 12 Questions

1. What must proceed spiritual growth?

2. What is another name for spiritual growth?

3. According to 1 Peter 2:2, what is needed for you to spiritually grow?

4. Is there anything wrong with being a babe in Christ? Why?

5. Is there something wrong with remaining a babe in Christ? Why?

6. Fill in the blank to complete the sentence: "God has provided everything necessary by His grace for you to grow as a child of God except for _____ _____."

7. Let's discuss God's grace design for growth. Fill in the blanks and answer the questions below.

    a. Spiritual growth takes _____. (Hebrews 5:12a)

    - Because this is true, we need to be _____ when it comes to our spiritual growth.

Your New Opportunity

    b. Spiritual growth takes _____. (Hebrews 5:12-13)

       • What is essential in your life to grow spiritually?

    c. Spiritual growth requires _____. (Hebrews 5:12-13; 1 Cor. 2:12)

       • Who is your inner and ultimate teacher of the Word of God? (1 Cor. 2:12)

       • Before you begin to read the Scriptures, what should you do? (Psalm 119:18)

       • Who are some of the human teachers that God is still providing today for believers to learn the Word of God? (Eph. 4:11-12)

       • Local churches are important for your spiritual growth; but what must you find out about a church before you start to attend regularly?

       • While you are in the process of finding a good local church in your area if this is possible, what might you do?

       • If you do find a sound, Bible-teaching church in your area, what should you do according to Hebrews 10:24-25?

d. Spiritual growth requires _____. (James 1:2-4)

- Why does God provide or allow trials or tests in our lives?

- When God allows trials in your life, what is He testing or refining?

- What is God also seeking to produce through the trial? (James 1:3)

- If we "know" these truths, how should we then respond in our trials?

- What is another reason God allows trials in our lives?

- Are trials a sign of God's displeasure in your life and reaping what you have sown?

- What is the point of the main story about the catfish in the codfish tank?

- Can you name a catfish or two in your life that God is seeking to use for your spiritual growth?

Your New Opportunity

- Look up Romans 8:28 and explain in your own words how this applies to the trials in your life?

- Look up 2 Corinthians 12:7-10 and explain what this teaches you about the trials and challenges in your life?

e. Spiritual grow requires _____. (Hebrews 11:6)

- Fill in the blanks: Hebrews 11:6 says, "Without _____ it is _____ to _____ Him [God], for He who comes to God must _____ that He is, and that He is a rewarder of them who _____ _____ Him."

- According to Hebrews 4:2, why did the Word not profit the past Exodus generation of Jews who heard it?

- How does a believer enter the spiritual rest of inner tranquility and peace that God desires His people to enjoy daily?

- Can you correctly state the 5 "Ts" in God's grace design for growth? Spiritual growth requires:

Chapter 13

YOUR NEW KEY TO FRUITFULNESS – ABIDING IN CHRIST

On the night before His crucifixion, our Lord Jesus Christ emphatically explained to His saved disciples (the only unbeliever, Judas, had already departed from them, John 13:30) exactly how to become a fruitful believer for Him after His departure. Using the analogy of a vine and branches, Jesus Christ stated,

> I am the true vine, and My Father is the vinedresser. Every branch in Me that does not bear fruit He takes away; and every branch that bears fruit He prunes, that it may bear more fruit. You are already clean because of the word which I have spoken to you. Abide in Me, and I in you. As the branch cannot bear fruit of itself, unless it abides in the vine, neither can you, unless you abide in Me. I am the vine, you are the branches. He who abides in Me, and I in him, bears much fruit; for without Me you can do nothing. (John 15:1-5)

Jesus Christ is likened to the "true vine"; God the Father is likened to the "vinedresser" or gardener; and believers in Christ are likened to "branches." Our Lord emphasizes and anticipates the position/identify in Christ of these believers as He describes them as "every branch *in Me*" (15:2a). We are again reminded that all fellowship, growth, and fruitfulness for Jesus Christ is first of all based on the work of Jesus Christ and our union with Him.

Next, we observe that while some believers are unfruitful (15:2a), God desires to produce in our lives "fruit" (15:2b) through abiding, "more fruit" through pruning (15:2c), and "much fruit" by abiding and pruning (15:5). Our Lord uses the concept of "fruit" because what He seeks to produce in our lives via the Holy Spirit (Gal. 5:22-23) is not the product of our self-effort and legalistic obedience but is the by-product of an effortless branch abiding in the vine so that the life and resources of the vine flow through the abiding branch, resulting in fruit. The term "fruit" in the New Testament is used to describe:

- Christ-like character (Gal. 5:22-23)
- Purposeful praise (Heb. 13:15)
- Generous giving (Phil. 4:15-17)
- Effective evangelism (John 4:36)
- Godly conduct (Col. 1:10)
- Meaningful ministry to others (Rom. 1:13)

But keep in mind that God never asked you to produce fruit but simply to "bear" it. This is where we are prone to become confused as we too often seek in our own wisdom or strength to produce fruit for God by our self-effort or works (see Paul in Romans 7:15-25). This is a certain recipe for spiritual failure, self-deception, or self-righteousness. But since the only human response consistent with God's grace is faith, the Scriptures make it clear that you are to live the Christian life each day in the same way that you were saved—by admitting you can't do it and instead by trusting daily in Jesus Christ to do it for you, in you, and through you as you "abide in Him."

> I have been crucified with Christ; it is no longer I who live, but Christ lives in me; and the life which I now live in the flesh I live by faith in the Son of God, who loved me and gave Himself for me. (Gal. 2:20)

> As you have therefore received Christ Jesus the Lord, so walk in Him, rooted and built up in Him and established in the faith, as you have been taught, abounding in it with thanksgiving. (Col. 2:6-7)
>
> For we walk by faith, not by sight. (2 Cor. 5:7)
>
> But without faith it is impossible to please Him, for he who comes to God must believe that He is, and that He is a rewarder of those who diligently seek Him. (Heb. 11:6)

This daily dependence upon the Lord is wonderfully expressed by the word "abide." The Greek word means to "remain or to stay." And where must the believer in Christ remain or stay in his thinking? The answer is, "Abide *in Me.*" In this context, "abide in Me" means to remain in dependence upon Jesus Christ instead of being independent of Him—like a branch must do with a vine if it is to be fruitful. You need to remember this in your thinking: the fruitful Christian life involves a daily, active dependence upon the Lord along with passive production—you don't produce its fruit for it is produced by Jesus Christ. All attempts to live the Christian life through self-effort (with God's supposed help) are doomed for failure and frustration. It is not a matter of "doing your best for Jesus" but Christ producing His best through you. Nor is it a matter of "wake up and get to work" for the Lord, though your labor is not in vain for the Lord and there is much labor for Christ that needs to be done. Instead the key to this involves the necessity of abiding in Christ for genuine fruitfulness and service to the Lord that honors Him (since He is the One who produces it in us and through us):

> *Abide in Me, and I in yo*u. As the branch *cannot* bear fruit of itself, *unless* it abides in the vine, *neither* can you, *unless* you abide in Me. I am the vine, you are the branches. He who abides in Me, and I in him, bears much fruit; *for without Me you can do nothing.* (John 15:4-5)

But what happens if you fail to walk with or depend upon Jesus Christ in your daily fellowship with Him as a result of sin or self-dependence?

> If anyone does not abide in Me, he is cast out as a branch and is withered; and they gather them and throw them into the fire, and they are burned. (John 15:6)

The word "if" indicates that you have a choice each day whether you will abide by faith in Christ or not. If you do not abide in Christ you will be disconnected from His fellowship ("cast forth as a branch"), your spiritual vitality and fruitfulness will "wither," and your life will be useless to God and for others just like fruitless branches that men burn. This may explain some believers you know, or perhaps even you! This verse does not warn of the loss of eternal salvation (as "eternal life" can never be lost) but the serious loss of fellowship, fruitfulness, and testimony that non-abiding believers can experience. But what instead does God want in your daily Christian walk?

> If you abide in Me, and My words abide in you, you will ask what you desire, and it shall be done for you. By this My Father is glorified, that you bear much fruit; so you will be My disciples. (John 15:7-8)

There is much false teaching today (even in evangelical Christianity that embraces the Bible as the Word of God) when it comes to being fruitful for Jesus Christ. So be forewarned of these various legalistic or mystical attempts at fruitbearing that bypass the necessity of simply abiding by faith in Jesus Christ in light of your position in Him.

Chapter 13 Questions

1. In Jesus' teaching of John 15, identify the three persons involved in the fruitbearing process.

2. What two important biblical truths are all fellowship, growth, and fruitfulness based upon?

3. Which member of the Trinity is needed to produce spiritual fruit in our lives?

4. Give some examples of spiritual fruit.

5. How does God want believers to bear fruit?

6. What does "abide in Christ" mean?

7. What happens if we as believers don't abide in Christ?

8. What are two false teachings that bypass the necessity of simply abiding by faith in Jesus Christ, in light of our position in Him?

Chapter 14

YOUR NEW ACCOUNTABILITY— THE JUDGMENT SEAT OF CHRIST!

The unsaved will one day be judged by Jesus Christ according to their works at the Great White Throne Judgment and then be cast into the Lake of Fire forever (Rev. 20:11-15). Why? It is because they trusted in their works instead of Jesus Christ to save them (John 3:18). This is a tragedy of eternal proportions. Yet there is also coming a day when every believer in Jesus Christ will stand before Him and give an account of how they lived their life as a new creation in Christ.

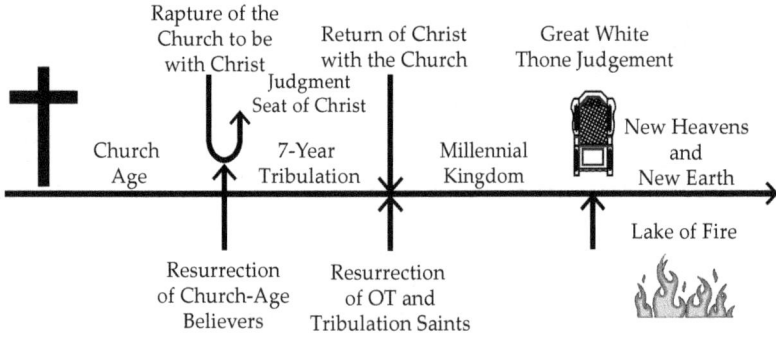

The purpose of this divine evaluation at the Judgment Seat of Christ (2 Cor. 5:9-10) is not to determine whether a person will go to Hell or Heaven. For you as a believer, that has been settled forever the moment you came to trust in the atoning work of Christ on the cross for you. You have eternal life from that moment on and you can also *"know* that you have eternal life" beyond the shadow of a doubt (1 John 5:13).

The purpose of the Judgment Seat of Christ is to reveal whether you have lived a life after being born again that honored Jesus Christ or not, and thus to determine whether you will receive a *reward* from the Lord or not. Yet do not be confused about this evaluation time. Heaven is NOT a reward for good people or for good works; it is a gift from God for guilty sinners who have placed their faith in Jesus Christ and His finished work on the cross to save them. But after you, as a believing sinner, have been saved eternally from sin's penalty and your destiny has been settled forever by God's grace, it is important to realize that God now has a plan for your life that includes "good works" as a result of becoming a new creation in Christ.

> For by grace you have been saved through faith, and that not of yourselves; it is the gift of God, not of works, lest anyone should boast. For we are His workmanship, *created in Christ Jesus for good works*, which God prepared beforehand that *we should walk in them*. (Eph. 2:8-10)

> [N]ot by works of righteousness which we have done, but according to His mercy He saved us, through the washing of regeneration and renewing of the Holy Spirit, whom He poured out on us abundantly through Jesus Christ our Savior, that having been justified by His grace we should become heirs according to the hope of eternal life. This is a faithful saying, and these things I want you to affirm constantly, that *those who have believed in God should be careful to maintain good works. These things are good and profitable to men.* (Titus 3:5-8)

THE PROPER PLACE OF GOOD WORKS

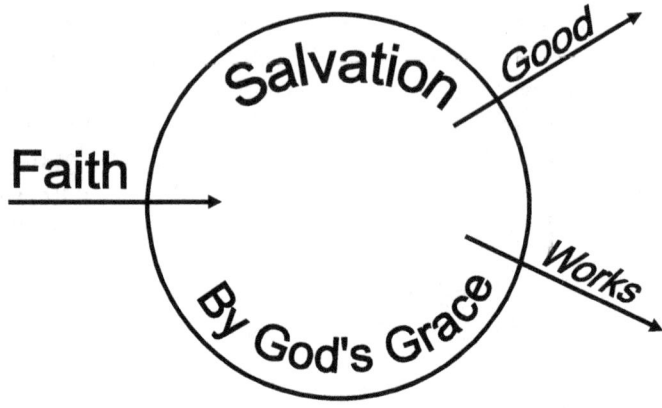

God has a personal plan for your Christian life to serve Jesus Christ that includes good works as a result of being saved by God's grace and learning now to walk daily by faith, in fellowship with the Lord, just like you were saved by faith (Gal. 2:20; Col. 2:6). Let's keep clear, however, that these good works God has planned for you are not *in order to go* to Heaven but because you are *already guaranteed* Heaven! These good works are not done now in order to be saved or kept saved but because you have been saved! These good works are not done to gain favor with God for you are already accepted in Christ by God's grace. Instead these good works are to be done by abiding in Christ and out of gratitude for Jesus Christ because of the grace blessings that you now have in Him. They are your personal "thank you" note for the great gift and blessings that God has lavished upon you in Christ. But unlike God's gift of salvation, these rewards are yet future and they can be either obtained or forfeited on the basis of the believer's faithfulness to the Lord or his lack thereof. For while some believers progress in their Christian lives and find great purpose and joy in serving the Lord, other believers waste their lives through self-indulgence and carnality which disappoints the Lord and delights Satan.

God guarantees the final salvation of every believer in Christ whether he receives a reward or not. So what is the significance of a reward? God desires that every believer knows His will (through His Word) and does His will (through the power of the Holy Spirit) for His glory. This is likened to a race where those who run and finish obtain a prize or crown.

> Do you not know that those who run in a race all run, but one receives the prize? Run in such a way that you may obtain it [the prize or reward; not the gift of salvation]. And everyone who competes for the prize is temperate in all things. Now they do it to obtain a perishable crown, but we for an imperishable crown. (1 Cor. 9:24-25)

God wants to reward each believer with a prize or crown for faithfully finishing the race of knowing and doing His will for his or her life. These rewards may include hearing one day "well done, good servant" (Luke 19:17), including "praise, honor, and glory at the revelation of Jesus Christ" (1 Peter 1:7). These rewards are also referred to in Scripture as different kinds of "crowns":

THREE CROWNS IN THE NEW TESTAMENT

| CROWN OF LIFE | CROWN OF RIGHTEOUSNESS | CROWN OF GLORY |

These future rewards and crowns will reflect the exact kind of service that you will render to the Lord in the Kingdom to come (Luke 19:11-27). The love of Christ, His finished work on the cross for you, and your new position in Christ should all act as great motivators for you to live for Him who died for you since you have been saved as a gift from God. In addition, the Judgment Seat of Christ and the scriptural truth of future rewards should remind you that it is truly worth it now and for all eternity to serve Jesus Christ as your Lord and not waste your opportunities to abide in and serve your Savior and Lord.

Chapter 14 Questions

1. Who will be judged by Jesus Christ at the Great White Throne Judgment?

2. On what basis will unbelievers be judged and what will be their destiny?

3. Why will every believer in Jesus Christ give an account to Jesus Christ?

4. What are God's purposes for the Judgment Seat of Christ?

5. Does the believer need to do good works to be saved or to be kept saved? Why or why not?

6. Does the believer in Christ need to do good works to gain favor from God? Why or why not?

7. What is the proper motivation for the believer in Christ to do good works for Jesus Christ?

8. Does God guarantee the final salvation of every believer whether he receives a reward or not?

9. Does every believer in Christ receive a reward?

10. Does God want to reward each believer with a prize or crown?

11. What are the three crowns specifically mentioned in the New Testament? List them, and then look them up and try to determine who is awarded these crowns in the corresponding Bible passages.

Chapter 15

YOUR NEW PROVISION FOR WHEN YOU FAIL—CONFESSION OF SIN!

Yes, Christians fail far more than some would like to admit. Sometimes they fail because in their pride they are convinced that their plan is better than God's. So instead of checking in with the Lord through His Word or in prayer, they launch out only to fail miserably or to seemingly succeed even more miserably. At other times believers fail because they are ignorant of the Scriptures, or walk in unbelief, believing the lies of Satan. At other times believers in Christ fail because they desire to do God's will but depend upon themselves to accomplish it (Rom. 7:15-18). They are like the apostle Peter who boldly proclaimed, "Lord, I am ready to go with You, both to prison and to death" (Luke 22:33). Notice the self-confidence in this statement instead of Christ dependence.

This is why our Lord replied to Peter, "I tell you, Peter, the rooster shall not crow this day before you will deny three times that you know Me" (Luke 22:34). Peter failed because though he wanted to do God's will, he lacked a sense of his own inadequacy and his need to depend upon Jesus Christ to fulfill it. And every spiritual failure you experience in your Christian life will be traced to these kinds of problems. This is why God wants to teach you every day the same essential truth you understood when you were saved: "Not that we are sufficient of ourselves to think of anything as being from ourselves, but our sufficiency is from God" (2 Cor. 3:5).

This verse is divided into two parts. The first half sets forth the reality that you are not sufficient in yourself to direct your life, build your marriage, fulfill your ministry, and address the needs of life. You can either take this by faith or learn this through your failures (the former is better than the latter). But just as you were insufficient to save yourself from the penalty of sin so that you trusted in Jesus Christ and His finished work to save you (and He did!), so now every day is a new opportunity to trust in the supremacy of Jesus Christ to direct your life and the sufficiency of Christ to live His life in and through you by the power of God's Spirit. What does God want from you? He desires a yielded attitude and a moment-by-moment trust in Jesus Christ and His power and promises.

It is so helpful when we finally realize that God is not looking for us to produce or perform the Christian life. He wants us to enjoy a vertical, invisible, personal fellowship with Him as His child forever. "That which we have seen and heard we declare to you, that you also may have *fellowship* with us; and truly our *fellowship is with the Father and with His Son Jesus Christ*. And these things we write to you that *your joy may be full*" (1 John 1:3-4).

Keep in mind that all believers in Christ have been born again into the family of God and have an eternal relationship with God. But this does not mean that every believer is enjoying daily "fellowship with God." In fact, some believers claim to be having fellowship with God while at the same time they are yielding to their sin natures and walking in sin. "If we say that we have *fellowship with Him*, and *walk in darkness, we lie* and *do not practice the truth*" (1 John 1:6). In stark contrast, the following verse states, "But *if we walk in the light* as He is in the light, *we have fellowship* with one another, and *the blood of Jesus Christ His Son cleanses us from all sin*" (1 John 1:7).

To "walk in the light" (as God is in the light) involves a willingness to walk by faith in the sphere of God's Word and truth so that you have "fellowship" with God, which then results in the blood of Jesus Christ having a cleansing effect upon your spiritual growth and practical sanctification. But you need to remember that fellowship with God does not require the loss of your sin nature or for you to reach a state of sinless perfection—both of which are impossible in this lifetime. For "If we say that we have no sin, we deceive ourselves, and the truth is not in us" (1 John 1:8). The denial of the fact that you still possess a sin nature even after you've been born again means you are deceiving yourself (and no one else) and God's truth is not in you. Although you still possess a sinful nature, victory over it is available through the cross (Rom. 6) and the Holy Spirit (Rom. 8). The awareness of an ever-present sin nature should keep you humble and dependent upon the Lord. But since we do not always appropriate God's grace by faith for practical victory and walk in His light, what is necessary when you fail and sin against the Lord and break fellowship with Him?

> If we confess our sins, He is faithful and just to forgive us our sins and to cleanse us from all unrighteousness. (1 John 1:9)

What God desires when He convicts you of sin is that you "confess" your known sins to Him (for how can you confess what you do not know?). To "confess" means to agree with God that what He says is indeed sin in your thinking, actions, tongue, or motives. For as any good relationship requires honest communication and admission when necessary, so does the believer's fellowship with God. Once you have confessed your sin to God, what does He promise to you? "He is faithful and just to forgive you your sins [i.e., the ones you have confessed] and cleanse you from all unrighteousness [i.e., the sins you have done ignorantly]." What grace! Notice that you do *not* need to *ask* God to forgive you and cleanse you as He has already promised to do so upon your honest confession of sin. But keep in mind that the purpose of your confession of sins is to yield to the Lord once again, and walk in the light by faith, and to have fellowship with God (1:7). Thus, upon confession of your sins to the Lord, you can claim God's total parental forgiveness, thank the Lord for His grace, know that your fellowship with God is instantly restored, and then move on by faith as Paul wrote, "forgetting those things that are behind, and reaching forward to those things which are ahead, I press toward the goal for the prize of the upward call of God in Christ Jesus" (Phil. 3:13-14).

Unfortunately, some believers walk by their feelings instead of by faith, not believing they are forgiven by God; or they "confess and try harder" instead of yielding to the Lord and walking by faith; or they scrutinize themselves constantly for sin and become very sin-focused instead of becoming Christ-focused and occupied; or they promise God they'll do better instead of faith-resting in God's promises; or they try to punish themselves instead of looking back to the cross in their minds where Jesus Christ was already punished for their sins. If the God of the universe has chosen to forgive your sins because of the blood of Christ, who are you to hold on to them after you've confessed them, as if they are not forgiven by God's grace?

The apostle John sets forth another possible wrong reaction by believers when the Holy Spirit convicts us of sin against the Lord: "If we say that we have not sinned, we make Him a liar, and His word is not in us" (1 John 1:10). You can either confess your sins to the Lord or cover your sins by excusing them, justifying yourself, or shifting the blame. When you choose to cover your sins, you continue walking in darkness, you do not have fellowship with God, and you will not progress in your spiritual growth. For "He who covers his sins will not prosper, but whoever confesses and forsakes them will have mercy" (Prov. 28:13). But remember that the purpose of this passage is not to abuse the grace of God by using 1 John 1:9 as an excuse for sinning, since the apostle writes, "My little children, these things I write to you, so that you may not sin" (1 John 2:1a).

Yet, God knows that there are times when we fail to walk in the light. Thus, John communicates great biblical balance and encouragement when he writes, "And if anyone sins, we have an Advocate with the Father, Jesus Christ the righteous. And He Himself is the propitiation for our sins, and not for ours only but also for the whole world" (1 John 2:1b-2). Dear friend, may you never lose sight of the fact that the holy God of the universe has been satisfied forever with Jesus Christ's payment for your sins made on the cross. And when Satan accuses you of sin (and there are many sins to point at), Jesus Christ defends you as your righteous advocate or defense attorney whose shed blood has met every holy demand against your sins. Praise the Lord!

Chapter 15 Questions

1. Does every believer automatically enjoy personal, daily "fellowship with God"?

2. Why do Christians fail?

3. How does a believer "walk in the light" (1 John 1:7)?

4. What does it mean to "confess" our sins (1 John 1:9)?

5. Once we have confessed to God, what does He promise to do according to 1 John 1:9?

6. What is the purpose of our confession? (1 John 1:7)

7. What can we claim once we have confessed our sins to the Lord?

8. What happens if you refuse to believe your sins are forgiven after you confess them?

9. What happens if you fail to confess your sins and cover them instead?

10. What does the Bible say that Jesus Christ does when Satan accuses you of sin?

Chapter 16

YOUR NEW WONDERFUL FUTURE IN CHRIST— THE BLESSED HOPE!

Since God promised you everlasting life the very moment you believed in Christ as Savior (John 3:16), you never need to fear death again as you did before you were saved (Heb. 2:14-15). So what happens at the moment of physical death for the believer?

> We are always confident, knowing that while we are at home in the body we are absent from the Lord. For we walk by faith, not by sight. We are confident, yes, well pleased rather to *be absent from the body and to be present with the Lord*. (2 Cor. 5:6-8)

The moment your soul and spirit become absent or separated from the body at physical death, you will be present with the Lord. There is no such thing in the Bible as "soul sleep" upon death, though your body will "sleep" in a figurative sense in the grave awaiting the day that it is resurrected and reunited with your redeemed soul. Because of this, the apostle Paul could state with certainty, "For to me, to live is Christ, and to die is gain. But if I live on in the flesh, this will mean fruit from my labor; yet what I shall choose I cannot tell. For I am hard pressed between the two, *having a desire to depart and be with Christ*, which is far better" (Phil. 1:21-23). Observe that to "depart" from this body for the believer means to "be with Christ." Thus, on the casket of every believer in Christ could be stamped the words, "far better." You as a child of God will then be with the Lord in Heaven enjoying salvation from the very presence of sin. There will even be a generation of believers in Christ that will never experience physical death but instead will receive a total bodily transformation.

> Behold, I tell you a mystery: *We shall not all sleep* [experience physical death], *but we shall all be changed—* in a moment, in the twinkling of an eye, at the last trumpet. For the trumpet will sound, and the *dead will be raised incorruptible, and we* [who have not died] *shall be changed*. (1 Cor. 15:51-52)

When does this bodily glorification occur for the dead in Christ and those believers in Christ who will not experience physical death? It is when the Lord returns for His Bride—the Church.

> But I do not want you to be ignorant, brethren, concerning those who have fallen asleep [believers who have physically died], lest you sorrow as others who have no hope. For if we believe that Jesus died and rose again [the Gospel], even so God will bring with Him those who sleep in Jesus. For this we say to you by the word of the Lord, that we who are alive and remain until the coming of the Lord will by no means precede those who are asleep [who have physically died in Christ]. For the Lord Himself will descend from heaven with a shout, with the voice of an archangel, and with the trumpet of God. And the dead in Christ will rise first [physical, bodily resurrection to be reunited with their redeemed souls]. Then we who are alive and remain [who have never experienced physical death] shall be caught up together [raptured] with them in the clouds to meet the Lord in the air. And thus we shall always be with the Lord. Therefore comfort one another with these words. (1 Thess. 4:13-18)

This is a win-win situation for the believer's future. If he or she dies before the return of the Lord, absent from the body means present with the Lord in Heaven. If the believer does not die before the Rapture (when the Lord snatches living believers in Christ from the earth), he or she is then caught up together with other believers in Christ to meet the Lord in the air! The result is that "we shall always be with the Lord"! No wonder Paul ends this passage by writing, "Therefore comfort one another with these words." Are you watching and waiting for the Lord's coming as it could be today? This is why the believer is to be "looking for the blessed hope and glorious appearing of our great God and Savior Jesus Christ" (Titus 2:13).

Chapter 16 Questions

1. What happens at the moment of physical death for the believer? (2 Cor. 5:6-8)

2. What will your body be awaiting upon death?

3. What could be stamped on the casket of every believer in Christ?

4. Why will there be a generation of believers in Christ that will never experience physical death?

5. What will happen "in the twinkling of an eye" to the generation of believers mentioned above?

6. With what words should we comfort one another as believers?

7. When could the Lord Jesus come back to resurrect and glorify believers, and what should we be doing in light of this?

8. How should we as believers view the Rapture in light of its description in Titus 2:13?

Chapter 17

YOUR NEW BEGINNING—IN CHRIST!

Let's summarize what you have read in this book, *I'm Saved! Now What?* We have studied regarding,

- YOUR NEW IDENTITY – "IN CHRIST"!
- YOUR NEW SPIRITUAL BLESSINGS IN CHRIST!
- YOUR NEW OPERATING PRINCIPLE – GOD'S GRACE!
- YOUR NEW SECURITY – SAVED AND SECURE FOREVER!
- YOUR NEW PRIMARY MOTIVATION – THE LOVE OF CHRIST!
- YOUR NEW PERSPECTIVE OF PEOPLE – IN ADAM OR IN CHRIST!
- YOUR NEW MINISTRY AND PRIVILEGE – AN AMBASSADOR FOR JESUS CHRIST!
- YOUR NEW MEANS OF COMMUNICATION WITH GOD – THE WORD OF GOD & BELIEVING PRAYER!

Your New Beginning

- **YOUR NEW UNDERSTANDING OF GOD'S PLAN FOR YOU – THE THREE TENSES OF SALVATION!**
- **YOUR NEW OPPORTUNITY – TO GROW SPIRITUALLY!**
- **YOUR NEW KEY TO FRUITFULNESS – ABIDING IN CHRIST!**
- **YOUR NEW ACCOUNTABILITY – THE JUDGMENT SEAT OF CHRIST!**
- **YOUR NEW PROVISION FOR WHEN YOU FAIL – CONFESSION OF SIN!**
- **YOUR NEW WONDERFUL FUTURE IN CHRIST – THE BLESSED HOPE!**

Dear child of God, you are a new creation in Christ with a wonderful new life to live and a new future to look forward to. May God be free to personally lead and guide you day by day as you learn to walk by faith and yield to the Lord, living in light of your new position in Christ. But let me also warn you that you can still choose to live a miserable life that dishonors the Lord, ruins your testimony for Christ, robs you of real inner joy and peace, and wastes your opportunities to serve Jesus Christ. Which will it be?

After I came to trust in Jesus Christ as my Savior, I was grateful for God's grace in saving me from a Hell that I deserved to a Heaven that I didn't. I was absolutely sure of my eternal destiny. I knew Christ's finished work on the cross and His resurrection from the grave were not only necessary but enough to save me. I was even willing to converse about spiritual things with others. But in my fleshly carnality, I still thought, "I'm glad I'm saved and going to Heaven, but I will take it from here Lord. I have my plans and objectives for life, and I can handle it." How foolish I was to think that I needed Jesus Christ to change only my eternal destiny but I didn't really need Him to direct my life from day to day. In my pride I thought I was sufficient in myself to tackle the trials and decisions of life. In my arrogance I thought I knew what was best for my life. But the Holy Spirit inside of me was convicting me as a believer of my stubbornness and rebellion. I was miserable and drowning my misery in various forms of escapism. The things of the world did not satisfy the yearnings of my soul as I had now tasted the grace of God (1 Peter 2:3) and fellowship with the Lord (1 John 1:3-4). As a child of God, my Heavenly Father lovingly disciplined me as promised (Heb. 12:5-11) largely by letting me just reap what I had sown by making a mess of my life. I felt like a fish out of water. I really didn't fit in any longer with my unsaved friends as I was a new creation in Christ. Yet, because of my carnality, I also didn't fit in with spiritual believers who wanted to live for Jesus Christ as I still wanted to live for the world (1 John 2:15-17). I was a consistently carnal believer for several months who was aimless and miserable, though on my way to Heaven by God's grace.

But thank God that the Lord still loved me, accepted me in Christ, and manifested His grace to me by letting me, just like the prodigal son, come to the end of myself (Luke 15:17). One night, I finally confessed my sins and yielded to the Lord to do His will. This resulted in real peace, joy, and purpose in my heart to live for Jesus Christ.

But even though I wanted to live for the Lord who redeemed me, I had no idea how to proceed or progress spiritually. Being raised in a kind and moral, but religious, home where the Gospel was not preached and the Word of God was not taught, my knowledge of the Scriptures was almost nonexistent. But God can work with a willing heart (which I now had). He graciously allowed me to have a Christian friend who also wanted to live for Jesus Christ and was farther along spiritually than myself. I greatly needed this since my unsaved friends soon forsook me as we were going in totally different directions in life (though I sought to maintain some contact with them and to give them the Gospel). In His grace, God also provided for me a Christ-centered, Bible-believing local church where I could hear the Gospel clearly, be fed the Word of God verse-by-verse, learn sound doctrine, and enjoy fellowship with other believers around the Lord. This was invaluable to my spiritual growth. I had so much to learn and so much for God to change, but He graciously kept bringing me along spiritually (Ps. 23:1-3).

Frankly, I had no plans or personal agenda to ever become a pastor. I was so unworthy to be used of the Lord in any way.

With the love of Christ compelling me, I just wanted to learn the Word of God and let my life now count for Jesus Christ. But God, in His grace (who also has a sense of humor), continued to spiritually mature me (remember the five "T"s of spiritual growth) and eventually called and prepared me years later to be used of Him in pastoral ministry. What a joy and privilege it has been! Yet for years I have sensed the need for a book or booklet of some kind to put into the hands of new or immature believers to personally encourage and doctrinally establish them in the wonderful truths of grace in all three tenses of salvation. Thus, may God be pleased by His grace to use the Word of God as presented in this short book to accomplish these divine purposes in your life for your good and His glory (Rom. 8:28-29). If this occurs in your life, give God the glory! Also feel free to write me with your joys and questions as I would love to be of any spiritual assistance to you. My email address is: dennis.rokser@gmail.com. Or you may write to me at:

Duluth Bible Church
c/o Dennis Rokser
201 W. St. Andrews St.
Duluth, MN 55803

I would encourage you to read this book over and over again until these truths become cemented in your thinking. Each time through it will make more and more sense as we learn, "line upon line, precept upon precept, here a little, there a little" (Isa. 28:10-11). In addition, you may want to read the next booklet in this developing series on the Christian life titled, *I'm Saved but Struggling with Sin! Is Victory Available?* (an explanation of Romans 6–8).

> Now may the God of peace who brought up our Lord Jesus from the dead, that great Shepherd of the sheep, through the blood of the everlasting covenant, make you complete in every good work to do His will, working in you what is well pleasing in His sight, through Jesus Christ, to whom be glory forever and ever. Amen. (Heb. 13:20-21)

CHAPTER QUESTIONS & ANSWERS

Chapter 1

1. What is the first issue between a sinner and God?

   Answer: There is first a need to have spiritual birth (being born again) that results in a change in eternal destiny (now having a home in Heaven).

2. What verse in the Bible capsulizes the main message of the Bible?

   Answer: John 3:16

3. Who is the subject of John 3:16? What is the context of John 3:16?

   Answer: Subject is God. Context: God is holy; man is sinful and separated from God.

4. What does it mean that God is holy?

   Answer: He is morally pure or perfect.

5. What did God give to man to express His holy commands?

   Answer: the Law, God's commandments

6. What is the wage or penalty for sin?

   Answer: Death or separation from God

Chapter Questions & Answers

7. Can your good works or religious rituals ever save you from Hell? Why or why not?

   Answer: No. It is because you would have to be perfectly good to go to Heaven, and no one qualifies.

8. Regarding the content of John 3:16, who does John 3:16 tell us about?

   Answer: Jesus Christ

9. Describe Jesus Christ. Is he a God or a man?

   Answer: He is God who also became a man.

10. For what purpose did Jesus Christ die?

    Answer: To fully pay the penalty of our sins and to remove the sin barrier

11. What is the proof that God accepted the substitutionary death of Christ as a complete payment for our sins?

    Answer: God raised Jesus from the dead.

12. What did Jesus mean when He cried out on the cross, "It is finished"?

    Answer: Our sins were paid in full

13. What is the only correct way to respond to the Gospel?

    Answer: to believe in Jesus Christ alone

14. By what means is a person not saved or born again?

    Answer: good works; religious rituals; a church or religion; repenting from one's sins; asking Jesus into your heart; etc.

15. What is "grace"?

    Answer: God's undeserved and unmerited kindness

16. Do people contribute anything to their spiritual birth? Would it be grace if you contributed some action or work to be born again?

    Answer: A person contributes nothing (just like in one's physical birth). It is because God provides it all on the basis of grace. It would not be by grace if you worked for it.

17. Is salvation an earned reward or a free gift?

    Answer: free gift

18. The one condition to receive the gift of salvation really needs to be clarified. Why is this needed so badly for so many people?

    Answer: Many people today who claim to be born again are confused about the sole condition for eternal life being simply faith alone in Christ alone.

19. What is the result of believing the Gospel?

    Answer: The one who believes in Christ alone for eternal salvation will not perish but now possesses eternal life.

20. When exactly does a person become born again and receive the gift of eternal life?

    Answer: the moment that person places his or her faith in Christ alone. However, not everyone knows the exact date when this transaction between the sinner and God transpires. What is important is that you have placed your faith in Christ period, not in Christ plus anyone or anything else.

21. Will the believer in Christ ever come into God's condemnation in the future? Why or why not?

    Answer: No, never, because Christ died for all sins. Therefore, the believer now has eternal life which lasts forever, and God promises that the one who has believed in Christ will not come into condemnation in the future.

Chapter Questions & Answers

22. How should the person who has received eternal life as a free gift logically respond toward God and Jesus Christ?

    Answer: With much thanks to God the Father for providing salvation for you, and to Jesus Christ for loving you and personally dying for your sins and being raised from the dead

23. If eternal salvation is this simple, what ultimately condemns a person to Hell? For help, see John 3:17-18.

    Answer: that person's failure to ever personally believe in Jesus Christ alone as Savior and be born again

24. Can a person know with 100-percent certainty that he/she has eternal life upon believing in Him alone? For help, see 1 John 5:11-13.

    Answer: YES! God promises eternal life to every believer in Christ based upon the finished work of Jesus Christ and the unfailing promises of God. So they can KNOW it with absolute certainty as God cannot lie.

25. Do you know for sure that you have eternal life? If not, why not settle the issue right now? Why not put your name in John 3:16 and believe the Gospel for yourself?

    Answer: For God so loved (Your Name), that He gave His only begotten Son to die for (Your Name) and be raised from the dead, that if (Your Name) believes in Him, (Your Name) should not perish in Hell, but (Your Name) will now and forever possess eternal life. Is this not good news from God to you?!

Chapter 2

1. Since every child of God needs a solid spiritual foundation, what is suggested that you do?

   Answer: Read this book through carefully, prayerfully, and repeatedly.

2. What does 2 Corinthians 5:15 state is true of all believers in Christ?
   Answer: They are new creations in Christ.

3. What does 2 Corinthians 5:17 mean?

   Answer: that God views you as a new creation in Christ because of your new birth

4. What does 2 Corinthians 5:17 not mean?

   Answer: It does not mean that your sin patterns have ceased or that your wrong thoughts and beliefs about things other than the Gospel have instantaneously changed.

5. What will be necessary to address these issues in your Christian life?

   Answer: ongoing spiritual growth after your spiritual birth

6. Why is it necessary to clarify 2 Corinthians 5:17?

   Answer: It is because an inaccurate understanding of this verse will lead to confusion and perhaps the undermining of a believer's assurance of eternal life as they now look at their Christian walk and works for assurance, instead of the finished work of Jesus Christ and the unfailing promises of God.

7. Observing the chart in this chapter, what things were true of you before you were saved, and what is true of you now because you are "in Christ"?

Answer: See the chart.

8. Using the Glossary of Terms and Definitions at the end of this book, look up the meaning of the various blessings you have in Christ as stated in the chart in this chapter (and discuss them in your study group).

9. If a believer is still living or struggling with sin in his/her life, does this mean that person was never saved or born again?

   Answer: NO! It simply means that believer needs to learn to walk with the Lord and grow spiritually.

10. What does "in Christ" refer to? And what is "all things become new" referring to?

    Answer: "In Christ" refers to the believer's new identity as one whom God now sees as being positionally in His Son, while "all things become new" refers to the believer's new position, possessions, and privileges in Christ, not to the pattern of that believer's daily walk or actions.

Chapter 3

1. Before you were saved, how did God view you in terms of your position or identity?

   Answer: He viewed me as being "in Adam."

2. What spiritual realities were true of you before you were "in Christ"?

   Answer: I was an unregenerate sinner who was spiritually dead and separated from God, part of the "Adam's family," and without God and without hope.

3. Who and what made the difference in your life spiritually?

   Answer: Jesus Christ and His blood

4. What does the "blood of Christ" refer to?

   Answer: His sacrificial death on the cross that paid the penalty for all sin

5. As a believer, how does God relate to you right now and for the rest of eternity?

   Answer: As a new creation, accepted in His Son, Jesus Christ

6. According to Ephesians 1:6, how does God "accept" you?

   Answer: Just as He does His very own Beloved Son

7. According to Ephesians 1:6, your incredible position in Christ magnifies and praises what aspect of God?

   Answer: His amazing grace

8. What does the poem at the end of the chapter mean to you personally?

   Answer: Answers will vary.

Chapter Questions & Answers

9. What kind of positive transformation will occur if believers begin to truly grasp how God now views them in Christ?

    Answer: Answers will vary.

10. Group discussion assignment: Look up the following verses and state what you observe about your position or identity in Christ. (Use the glossary of terms and definitions as needed.) Answers will vary.

    a. 1 Corinthians 15:22

    b. Ephesians 1:3

    c. Ephesians 1:6

    d. Ephesians 1:7

    e. Ephesians 1:13

    f. Ephesians 2:4-7

    g. Ephesians 2:8-9

    h. Ephesians 2:10

    i. Ephesians 2:11-13

Chapter 4

1. According to Ephesians 1:3, what is now true of every believer "in Christ"?

   Answer: He/she has been blessed with every spiritual blessing in the heavenly places in Christ.

2. According to Colossians 2:10, what also is true of those "in Christ"?

   Answer: The believer is "complete" in Christ.

3. How can the illustration of a newborn baby assist you to grasp what Ephesians 1:3 and Colossians 2:10 mean as they relate to your possessions in Christ and spiritual growth?

   Answer: Like a baby, you were born again complete in Christ with all spiritual blessings. Now you just need to spiritually grow with what you already possess.

4. What does a failure to understand your completeness in Christ lead people to falsely teach or believe?

   Answer: That believers need some counterfeit ecstatic, mystical experiences.

5. How do Luke 9:58, 1 Corinthians 4:8-14, and Philippians 2:25-30 prove the sufficiency of your spiritual position and blessings in Christ?

   Answer: Jesus, the apostles, and first-century believers were mistreated and physically and materially poor, but they were spiritually rich.

6. This chapter has a partial listing of the believer's blessings or possessions in Christ. Look up some (below) or all the verses if you have time, in your Bible. You may use your Glossary of Terms and Definitions at the back of this book to understand the meaning of some of these biblical words.

Chapter Questions & Answers

John 19:30 – The penalty for my sins has been paid completely.

John 5:24 – I have passed from spiritual death into spiritual life.

Colossians 1:12 – I have been made fit for my future home in Heaven.

Ephesians 1:7 – I have the judicial forgiveness of all past, present, and future sins.

Colossians 1:13 – I have been delivered from the power of darkness into God's light.

John 3:7 – I have been renewed and regenerated by the Holy Spirit.

John 1:12 – I am a child of God.

Ephesians 2:5 – I have been seated in heavenly places with Christ.

Hebrews 13:15-16 – I am a priest who can offer spiritual sacrifices to God.

1 Corinthians 6:19 – My body is the temple of the Holy Spirit.

Romans 6:2 – I died to the sin nature.

Philippians 3:20 – I am a citizen of Heaven.

Hebrews 11:13; 1 Peter 2:11 – I am a stranger and a pilgrim who is no longer at home in this world.

Romans 5:1 – I have peace with God.

John 14:2 – I have a place in Heaven reserved for me.

Revelation 2:11 – I will not be hurt by the second death (eternal hell).

Revelation 21:3-4 – I will be with God forever.

7. Read out loud this list as you marvel at the riches of God's grace to you. If this is a group study, you can have each person in turn read out loud the blessings on the list until every blessing has been stated.

8. When do these spiritual blessings become the believer's present and eternal possession?

    Answer: At the moment of salvation or the new birth; otherwise, not every believer would be complete in Christ as some would be waiting for "something more"

9. Spiritual ignorance is not bliss but a serious blunder for every child of God. Does God want believers in Christ to be ignorant of their position and their spiritual blessings in Christ?

    Answer: No, God wants all believers to KNOW of their position and possessions in Christ.

10. To understand better what God wants for you as a new believer, read Ephesians 1:3, followed by 1:15-23. Also, God wants you to live with the awareness of your blessings in Christ Jesus each day. Read Ephesians 4:1-3.

11. Where will you read and learn about your riches in Christ?

    Answer: Only in the Bible

12. Why not end this session by pausing to praise and thank God in prayer for some or all of these wonderful blessings in Christ that He has given you because of the finished work of Christ and the riches of His amazing grace?

Chapter Questions & Answers

Chapter 5

1. What is the primary definition of "grace" (charis)?

   Answer: God's unmerited, undeserved kindness or blessing

2. Why does God deal with man in such amazing grace?

   Answer: It is because of who God is and what Jesus Christ has done for us.

3. Look up and read Isaiah 55:8-11. Do we naturally think according to God's grace?

   Answer: No

4. What observations can you make when reading Romans 11:6, Romans 4:4-5, and Ephesians 2:8-9?

   Answer: Various observations may be made but clearly there is a contrast between grace versus works.

5. Go back and read Romans 4:5 and Ephesians 2:8-9, along with Acts 10:43, 13:38-39, 16:30-31, and Romans 3:28. What is the only human response consistent with God's grace?

   Answer: It is faith in Jesus Christ alone.

6. How is God described in 1 Peter 5:10?

   Answer: He is described as "the God of all grace."

7. Look up the following verses and observe what each one teaches you regarding God's grace (Romans 5:1-2; 2 Peter 3:18; 1 Cor. 15:10; Hebrews 13:9; 2 Cor. 12:7-9).

   Answers:
   Romans 5:2 – You have access into God's grace.
   2 Peter 3:18 – You are to grow in grace.
   1 Corinthians 15:10 – You are what you are by God's grace, and His grace also enables you to serve Him.

Hebrews 13:9 – You need to become established in sound doctrine by grace.

2 Corinthians 12:7-9 – Instead of removing trials from our lives, God wants us to learn that His grace is sufficient for us to face every trial and go through them.

8. Look up Revelation 1:3; Romans 10:17; 2 Timothy 2:15; and Acts 20:32. How does a believer become established in the truths of God's grace?

   Answer: It is by reading, hearing, studying, and believing God's Word.

9. What are some recommendations when a believer first starts reading the Bible?
   Answer:
   - Read first the Gospel of John, observing the number of times the word "believe" is used as the only condition for eternal life.
   - Read Romans through the rest of the New Testament. (Don't expect to understand everything at once but enjoy what you do understand.)
   - Listen to the following messages by Dennis Rokser online: "It is Finished" - https://www.youtube.com/watch?v=vou9GhnrUb4
   "The Wonder of Calvary" -https://www.sermonaudio.com/sermoninfo.asp?SID=41809157500
   - Read the book *By This Name* by John Cross. You may want to read this book before you read through John Gospel since it takes you from Creation (in the book of Genesis) through the resurrection of Jesus Christ (in the New Testament), putting in place a lot of the pieces of the biblical puzzle for the reader. (Read online at http://av.goodseed.com/books/en/BTN_web.pdf
   - Download and read the pdf version of the booklet, *John 3:16 Illustrated* (www.gracegospelpress.org/free-downloads/), and watch the video "John 3:16 Fair Diagram

Chapter Questions & Answers

Explained" (https://www.youtube.com/watch?v=-w8s-6WymPw4)

10. What can you learn about God's grace and prayer from Hebrews 4:14-16?

    Answer: God wants you to come boldly and as needed to His throne of grace to obtain mercy and find grace to help in time of your need. (Why not end this session by doing just that?)

Chapter 6

Fill in the blank and answer the following questions.

1. God declares that you are a <u>child of God forever</u>. (John 1:12)

   a. Like your physical birth, what is true of your spiritual birth?

   Answer: It is a non-repeatable, once-for-all event that cannot be undone.

   b. What two scriptural concepts must you keep clear in your thinking?

   Answer: Entering the family of God and enjoying daily fellowship with God.

   c. How often does entrance into the family of God occur?

   Answer: once for all at a moment of time

   d. How often is fellowship with God to occur?

   Answer: It is to occur daily, step by step, moment by moment as you learn to walk by faith.

   e. What does sin in the life of the believer break?

   Answer: Fellowship with God.

   f. What does unconfessed sin in the life of the believer bring upon himself/herself?

   Answer: It brings God's loving, divine discipline or chastisement.

   g. Does sin in the life of the child of God cause him/her to lose his/her salvation? Why?

   Answer: No, it is because all of the believer's sins were

paid for by Christ and positonally forgiven the moment of faith alone in Christ alone.

h. Observe the chart on the Family of God and Fellowship with God and fill in the blanks below.

Once a person has placed his faith alone in <u>Christ</u> alone (John 1:12), he is forgiven of all sins and is placed in the <u>family</u> of God (Gal. 3:26). At the same time, the believer is also <u>baptized</u> by the Holy Spirit and becomes part of the body of Christ (1 Cor. 12:13). Although the believer will never be removed from the family of God, he must consistently confess his sins to remain in <u>fellowship</u> with God (1 John 1:3-10).

2. God promises you that every believer in Christ <u>presently possesses eternal life</u>. (John 3:16)

   a. What verb tense is the word "have" in John 3:16?
   Answer: It is the present tense.

   b. What does the word "have" mean?
   Answer: to presently possess

   c. How long does "everlasting life" last?
   Answer: Forever!

   d. If this is true, can your new birth be undone later by sin in your Christian life, unfaithfulness, or carnality? Why?
   Answer: No! Otherwise, the words "have everlasting life" would mean nothing and God would be a liar.

3. God declares that you either <u>possess eternal life</u> or else <u>you never possessed</u> it. (John 3:36)

   a. What is God's promise to the one who "believes in the Son"?

   Answer: He presently and forever "has everlasting life."

   b. What is God's two-fold evaluation about the one "who does not believe the Son"?

   Answer: He "shall not see (everlasting) life, but the wrath of God abides on him."

   c. What does this indicate about possessing everlasting life?

   Answer: Either one has everlasting life or they have never had it.

4. God has promised that you are guaranteed <u>never to come into future condemnation</u>. (John 5:24)

   a. According to John 5:24, what 3 things does God promise to give the person who believes God's Word?

   Answer:
   - "has everlasting life"
   - "shall not come into condemnation [judgment]"
   - "but has passed from [spiritual] death into [spiritual] life"

   b. If a believer could lose his/her salvation through sin, unfaithfulness, carnality, or apostasy, how would these promises be contradicted by God (who cannot lie)?

   Answer:
   - He would lose "everlasting life."
   - He would "come into condemnation."
   - He would pass from spiritual "life" to spiritual "death."

Chapter Questions & Answers

5. God has promised that you will <u>never be cast out of His family</u>. (John 6:35-37)

    a. What does Christ promise will never happen to the person who comes to Him by faith alone?

    Answer:
    - He "shall never hunger" (for everlasting life or an eternal relationship with God).
    - He "shall never thirst."
    - Christ will never "cast him out."

    b. If a believer could lose his salvation, how would these promises be contradicted by God (who cannot lie)?

    Answer:
    - He would spiritually "hunger" again.
    - He would spiritually "thirst" again.
    - He would be "cast out" of God's family.

    c. What can you conclude from these wonderful and unfailing promises of God that include the word "never"?

    Answer: Salvation or eternal life can never be lost under any circumstances or conditions.

6. God has promised that in Christ you will <u>never be lost again</u>. (John 6:38-40)

    a. What is the three-fold promise of Jesus Christ to the believer in Him?

    Answer:
    - Jesus Christ "will lose nothing."
    - Jesus Christ promises them "everlasting life."
    - Jesus Christ promises that "I will raise him up at the last day."

b. If Jesus Christ will lose nothing, and the believer has everlasting life with the guarantee of a future bodily resurrection, what can you conclude from this?

Answer: The believer in Christ can never lose his/her eternal salvation.

7. God has promised that you will never perish, nor ever be snatched out of Christ's or the Father's hands. (John 10:28-30)

   a. What are the four promises that Jesus Christ gives to those who "follow" (trust in) Him like a sheep with a shepherd?

   Answer:
   - Jesus Christ gives them "eternal life."
   - Jesus Christ promises "they shall never perish."
   - Jesus Christ guarantees that "no one shall snatch them out of My hand."
   - Jesus Christ promises that "no one is able them out of My Father's hand."

   b. If a believer could lose his salvation through sin, a lack of holiness, unfaithfulness, etc., how would these promises be contradicted by God (who cannot lie)?

   Answer:
   - He would lose eternal life.
   - He would perish.
   - He would escape out of Christ's hand.
   - He would escape out of the Father's hand.

   c. If a believer could do something to lose his salvation, what would he be required to do?

   Answer: He would have to do something to keep it.

   d. If a believer was required to do something to stay saved or not lose eternal life, would salvation then depend on God or the believer?

   Answer: The believer

Chapter Questions & Answers

e. If salvation was dependent upon the believer's walk, faithfulness, holiness, not sinning, ongoing confession of sin, perseverance, etc., would salvation be based upon God's grace or the believer's works?

   Answer: It would not be by God's grace but the believer's works.

f. How would this conclusion contradict Ephesians 2:8-9, and who then could the believer boast in?

   Answer: Salvation would then not be through faith alone but faith plus a person's works, which means salvation would be earned or merited and not by grace. It would be a reward, not a gift from God, and one could boast in what he has done instead of boasting in Christ alone.

g. If believers could somehow lose their salvation through sin, unfaithfulness, carnality, apostasy, etc., could they know for sure that they have eternal life and will go to Heaven when they die?

   Answer: No, unless they are self-deceived or arrogant enough to think they are worthy of Heaven due to their holy walk, true-blue faithfulness, total repentance of sin, etc.

h. According to 1 John 5:13, what does God assure those who believe in the name of the Son of God?

   Answer: God promises that "they may know that they have eternal life."

i. According to Romans 8:38-39, what can every believer be persuaded of?

   Answer: That no one and nothing can separate them from the love of God which is in Christ Jesus our Lord.

j. Is there any conditions or circumstances missing from God's perspective that could ever separate the believer from the love of God in Christ Jesus?

   Answer: No!

k. Are you persuaded that you are now and forever eternally secure in Christ?

   Answer: Answers will vary.

Chapter Questions & Answers

Chapter 7

1. What is NOT a scriptural reason to serve the Lord after a sinner has been saved? Why?

   Answer: The Fear of Hell, because no believer ever needs to fear Hell again because he has eternal life and God has promised he shall never perish.

2. What are three great motivators now to live for Jesus Christ once a person is saved?

   Answer: They are the love of Christ, the work of Calvary, and the believer's new position or identity in Christ.

3. Can you identify these three great motivations to live for Christ in 2 Corinthians 5:14-15?

   Answer:
   a. The love of Christ compels us.
   b. He died for all of us and we are now no longer in bondage (we are dead) to our old sin nature.
   c. We should no longer live for ourselves, but instead for Jesus who died for us and rose again.

4. Instead of being motivated by God's law, what should now motivate the believer in Christ?

   Answer: God's love!

5. Instead of being motivated by guilt or obligation, what should now motivate the believer in Christ?

   Answer: God's grace!

6. How does God now view the believer in light of the death and resurrection of Jesus Christ and your identity / position in Him?

   Answer: The believer has died with Christ and has been raised with Him.

7. Can you state two more passages of Scripture that support the love of Christ as a key motivator now to walk with Him and love Him?

   Answer: Galatians 2:20; 1 John 4:19.

8. Complete this verse: "For to me to live is <u>Christ</u>, and to die is <u>gain</u>." (Phil. 1:21)

9. What does the illustration of the slave auction in New Orleans years ago set forth?

   Answer: How a tremendous act of love in purchasing the slave woman and setting her free resulted in great gratitude for the man who did this for her, motivating her to want to serve him willingly.

10. Have you decided to live for Jesus Christ who died for you and rose again?

    Answer: Answers will vary.

11. Why don't believers in Christ choose to live daily for Jesus Christ?

    Answer: Answers will vary.

12. What are some other valid, biblical motivations to live for the Lord as a believer?

    Answer: Answers will vary, but here are a few reasons:
    a. To enjoy fellowship with the Lord (1 John 1:3-4)
    b. To become transformed by the Holy Spirit to be more like Christ (Rom. 5:3-4; 8:29; 2 Cor. 3:18; Gal. 4:19)
    c. To represent Christ to others as His ambassador and a loving witness to them (2 Cor. 5:20; 2 Tim. 2:10)
    d. To gain an eternal reward (2 Tim. 4:7-8; Heb. 11:35; James 1:12)
    e. To glorify God for He is worthy (1 Cor. 10:31; 2 Cor. 4:15-16)

Chapter Questions & Answers

Chapter 8

1. As a result of becoming a new creation in Christ, God wants to transform the thinking of believers through His Word so that they no longer view other people from what perspective?

   Answer: From the perspective of human standards, opinions, reasoning, etc.

2. How does God want believers now to view others?

   Answer: From His standard of people's identification with either Adam or Christ.

3. As believers view people from a new creation perspective, what questions will they now take into consideration?

   Answer: They will now take into consideration people's response and relationship to Jesus Christ and the Gospel.

4. How should these truths move us practically toward the unsaved?

   Answer: It should cause us to have a deep concern for their salvation.

Chapter 9

1. When you were saved by God's grace through faith alone in Christ alone, what was a major reason God did not take you home immediately to Heaven?

   Answer: Because God wants to use you as an ambassador for Jesus Christ to share the Gospel with others.

2. Does God want all sinners to be saved and to come to the knowledge of the truth of the Gospel?

   Answer: YES! (Read 1 Timothy 2:4)

3. For God to accomplish the reconciliation of sinners to Himself based on the finished work of Jesus Christ, what does God now want to do with saved sinners?

   Answer: He wants to use believers as heralds of the message of salvation so others could hear, believe, and be saved.

4. What spiritual truth is pictured by the metaphor of believers being "ambassadors" for Jesus Christ?

   Answer: As believers in Christ, we are living in foreign territory as representatives of the King, with a message to faithfully proclaim to the inhabitants of that land.

5. What does the truth of being an "ambassador for Christ" mean to you personally?

   Answer: Answers will vary.

6. While you may be untrained in evangelism and afraid to witness for Christ, what are some things that you can do right now?

   Answer: You can pray for the lost; you could give people appropriate Gospel literature such as the booklets *John 3:16 Illustrated, You Must Be Born Again, The Tale of Two Thieves, What Cancer Cannot Do,* etc.

Chapter Questions & Answers

7. What is another extremely helpful resource to watch and learn how to present the Gospel to others?

    Answer: You can watch how to present the Gospel by explaining John 3:16 at: www.youtube.com/watch?v=-w8s6WymPw4

8. Can you explain the "great exchange" according to 2 Corinthians 5:21?

    Answer: God the Father took all our sins and imputed them to His Son, Jesus Christ, who was judged with the death we deserved by dying in our place, so that when we believed in Jesus Christ, His righteousness was imputed or credited to us by God on the basis of His grace and the satisfactory death of His Son.

9. Since our time on earth is short and eternity is long, what should believers seek to do?

    Answer: To redeem the time with a pilgrim mentality and seek to capture the opportunities to serve Christ and make Him known.

10. If you are in a group, go around the group and take some time to discuss your burdens for the lost you know, writing down their names and praying for them.

Chapter 10

1. Is true Christianity a "religion"?

   Answer: No, it is a relationship with God of divine accomplishment.

2. As a result of being born again, what are three spiritual realities that God wants to occur in your life as a believer?

   Answer: To grow spiritually; to walk by faith; and to enjoy sweet fellowship with the Lord

3. How does the analogy of a new-born baby relate to your spiritual growth as a believer? (1 Peter 2:2)

   Answer: Believers are to have an intense desire for the milk of God's Word to grow.

4. In light of the believer's need to learn sound, biblical teaching, what are some recommendations?

   Answer: A good study Bible; a truly Bible-teaching and Gospel-preaching church; pray for wisdom and God's leading; online studies

5. How does God speak to you today?

   Answer: Through the reading, studying, and memorizing of His Word

6. Fill in the blanks: Jesus Christ said, "Man shall not live on bread <u>alone</u>, but by every <u>word</u> that proceeds from the <u>mouth of God</u>." (Matthew 4:4)

7. Being likened to a mirror, what does God use to transform believers internally by the Holy Spirit?

   Answer: The Word of God

Chapter Questions & Answers

8. According to Psalm 119:9-11, how does God want to use His Word in the believer's life?

    Answer: To cleanse his way and keep him from sin

9. According to Psalm 119:105, what is another benefit of learning the Word of God?

    Answer: To provide direction for your life path

10. Does God ideally want a monologue or a dialogue with His children? How is this possible?

    Answer: A dialogue – through hearing God via His Word and talking to God in prayer

11. What are four elements to include in your prayer to God?

    Answer: Praise; thanksgiving; admission or confession of sin; and making requests for yourself and others

Chapter 11

1. How many phases, stages, or tenses are involved in God's plan of salvation? (Study the chart at the beginning of the chapter.)

   Answer: Three

2. What aspect of sin were you saved from the moment you placed your faith in Christ as Savior?

   Answer: The penalty of sin, which is eternal death

3. Fill in the blanks: For by <u>grace</u> you <u>have been</u> saved through <u>faith</u>, and that not of yourselves; it is the <u>gift</u> of God. (Ephesians 2:8-9)

4. What aspect of sin does God now want to save / deliver you from daily?

   Answer: The power of sin

5. Why is this "salvation" needed in your daily Christian life?

   Answer: Because you still have a sin nature inside of you that wants to rule your life and lead you into various patterns of sin

6. What does God now want you to know regarding the sin nature's right to rule in your life?

   Answer: That it has been stripped of its past authority (read Romans 6:1-14)

7. Why else is salvation from sin's power needed in our lives?

   Answer: Because of the human viewpoint and worldly thinking that needs to be replaced with God's viewpoint from His Word

Chapter Questions & Answers

8. What are two ways that Satan seeks to hinder your spiritual growth in Christ?

    Answer: persecution and worldly distraction (read Luke 8:13-15)

9. What aspect of deliverance from sin does the third phase or stage of God's plan of salvation for you involve?

    Answer: salvation from sin's presence

10. Is this phase of salvation guaranteed and where will it ultimately be experienced?

    Answer: Yes! In Heaven

11. Can you remember the 3 phases or tenses of salvation for the believer in Christ?

    Answer:
    I have been saved from sin's penalty.

    I am being saved from sin's power.

    I will be saved from sin's presence.

Chapter 12

1. What must proceed spiritual growth?
   Answer: Spiritual birth

2. What is another name for spiritual growth?
   Answer: Progressive sanctification

3. According to 1 Peter 2:2, what is needed for you to spiritually grow?
   Answer: To desire the pure milk of God's Word

4. Is there anything wrong with being a babe in Christ? Why?
   Answer: No. All believers begin there.

5. Is there something wrong with remaining a babe in Christ? Why?
   Answer: Yes, because God wants every believer to mature.

6. Fill in the blank to complete the sentence: "God has provided everything necessary by His grace for you to grow as a child of God except for _____ _____."
   Answer: "God has provided everything necessary by His grace for you to grow as a child of God except for the faith you must learn to exercise in daily dependence on Him and His promises."

7. Let's discuss God's grace design for growth. Fill in the blanks and answer the questions below.

   a. Spiritual growth takes <u>Time</u>. (Hebrews 5:12a)

   - Because this is true, we need to be <u>patient</u> when it comes to our spiritual growth.

Chapter Questions & Answers

b. Spiritual growth takes <u>Truth</u>. (Hebrews 5:12-13)

- What is essential in your life to grow spiritually?

    Answer: The regular intake of the milk and meat of God's Word

c. Spiritual growth requires <u>Teachers</u>. (Hebrews 5:12-13; 1 Cor. 2:12)

- Who is your inner and ultimate teacher of the Word of God? (1 Cor. 2:12)

    Answer: The Holy Spirit

- Before you begin to read the Scriptures, what should you do? (Psalm 119:18)

    Answer: Pray for understanding and enlightenment.

- Who are some of the human teachers that God is still providing today for believers to learn the Word of God? (Eph. 4:11-12)

    Answer: Evangelists, pastors, and teachers

- Local churches are important for your spiritual growth; but what must you find out about a church before you start to attend regularly?

    Answer: Whether they preach the Gospel clearly and accurately or not. This is the starting point.

- While you are in the process of finding a good local church in your area if this is possible, what might you do?

    Answer: Contact the person or church that gave you this book.

- If you do find a sound, Bible-teaching church in your area, what should you do according to Hebrews 10:24-25?

  Answer: Not avoid regularly attending church

d. Spiritual growth requires <u>Trials</u>. (James 1:2-4)

- Why does God provide or allow trials or tests in our lives?

  Answer: To motivate us to learn and give us opportunity to apply God's Word

- When God allows trials in your life, what is He testing or refining?

  Answer: Our faith

- What is God also seeking to produce through the trial? (James 1:3)

  Answer: Patience

- If we "know" these truths, how should we then respond in our trials?

  Answer: We should still find joy in the Lord amidst these trials.

- What is another reason God allows trials in our lives?

  Answer: To make us mature and spiritually balanced

- Are trials a sign of God's displeasure in your life and reaping what you have sown?

  Answer: No. They are sometimes because of the curse stemming from Adam's sin.

- What is the point of the main story about the catfish in the codfish tank?

Chapter Questions & Answers

> *Answer:* God uses trials to keep us turning to Him and to prevent us from growing soft.

- Can you name a catfish or two in your life that God is seeking to use for your spiritual growth?

  Answer: Answers will vary.

- Look up Romans 8:28 and explain in your own words how this applies to the trials in your life?

  Answer: In God's sovereignty, He may allow even bad circumstances to accomplish something good in our Christian lives.

- Look up 2 Corinthians 12:7-10 and explain what this teaches you about the trials and challenges in your life?

  Answer: God's grace is always sufficient in every trial.

e. Spiritual grow requires <u>Trust</u>. (Hebrews 11:6)

- Fill in the blanks: Hebrews 11:6 says, "Without _____ it is _____ to _____ Him [God], for He who comes to God must _____ that He is, and that He is a rewarder of them who _____ _____ Him."

  Answer: Hebrews 11:6 says, "Without <u>faith</u> it is <u>impossible</u> to <u>please</u> Him [God], for He who comes to God must <u>believe</u> that He is, and that He is a rewarder of them who <u>diligently</u> <u>seek</u> Him."

- According to Hebrews 4:2, why did the Word not profit the past Exodus generation of Jews who heard it?

  Answer: They did not mix God's Word with personal faith.

- How does a believer enter the spiritual rest of inner tranquility and peace that God desires His people to enjoy daily?

    Answer: It is by knowing and believing His promises so that we stop trying to help God out and rest by faith in His plan and promises to us.

- Can you correctly state the 5 "Ts" in God's grace design for growth? Spiritual growth requires:

    Answer: Time, Truth, Teachers, Trials, and Trust

Chapter 13

1. In Jesus' teaching of John 15, identify the three persons involved in the fruitbearing process.

   Answer: The Vinedresser refers to God the Father; the True Vine refers to Jesus Christ; and the branches are believers in Jesus Christ.

2. What two important biblical truths are all fellowship, growth, and fruitfulness based upon?

   Answer: They are based on the work of Jesus Christ and our union with Him.

3. Which member of the Trinity is needed to produce spiritual fruit in our lives?

   Answer: The Holy Spirit

4. Give some examples of spiritual fruit.

   Answer: Christ-like, godly behavior; praise to God; giving; evangelism; and ministry to help others

5. How does God want believers to bear fruit?

   Answer: He wants us not to produce fruit or seek to be fruitful in our own strength or self-effort (in the flesh) but by admitting we can't do it and trusting in Christ to do it for us as we abide in Him.

6. What does "abide in Christ" mean?

   Answer: It means to remain in daily, active dependence on the Lord and allowing Jesus Christ to produce the fruit, instead of living the Christian life through our own self-efforts.

7. What happens if we as believers don't abide in Christ?

   Answer: Though we can never lose our salvation or position in the family of God as children of God, if we don't abide in Christ we lose fellowship with God, spiritual joy and vitality, and we may lose our testimony to others.

8. What are two false teachings that bypass the necessity of simply abiding by faith in Jesus Christ, in light of our position in Him?

   Answer: Legalism and mysticism. Legalism is the mental attitude that seeks to earn or merit the blessings of God by keeping religious rules or doing religious rituals or good works, either for eternal salvation or sanctification. Mysticism is a false belief that encourages people to possess a deeper or higher spiritual state based on personal subjective feelings, experiences, inward tuitions, or extra-biblical revelations.

Chapter Questions & Answers

Chapter 14

1. Who will be judged by Jesus Christ at the Great White Throne Judgment?

   Answer: The Unsaved

2. On what basis will unbelievers be judged and what will be their destiny?

   Answer: They will be judged according to their own works because they never trusted in Christ's work to saved them; thus, they will be cast into the Lake of Fire forever.

3. Why will every believer in Jesus Christ give an account to Jesus Christ?

   Answer: We will still give an account to Jesus Christ for how we lived our life after we were born again, whether we lived for ourselves or sought to live for Him.

4. What are God's purposes for the Judgment Seat of Christ?

   Answer: To reveal whether we have lived for a life (after being born again) that honored Jesus Christ, and to determine what reward (if any) we will receive from Him.

5. Does the believer need to do good works to be saved or to be kept saved? Why or why not?

   Answer: No, the believer does not need to do good works, because the believer has been saved forever and is permanently guaranteed a place in Heaven.

6. Does the believer in Christ need to do good works to gain favor from God? Why or why not?

   Answer: No, the believer does not need to do good works to gain favor from God because he or she is already accepted in Christ by God's grace.

7. What is the proper motivation for the believer in Christ to do good works for Jesus Christ?

   Answer: Out of gratitude for Jesus Christ, as a personal "thank you" note for the great gift and blessings He has lavished upon us in Christ by His grace.

8. Does God guarantee the final salvation of every believer whether he receives a reward or not?

   Answer: Yes, He does!

9. Does every believer in Christ receive a reward?

   Answer: No, he or she does not.

10. Does God want to reward each believer with a prize or crown?

    Answer: Yes, He really does want to reward us for serving Him, which is why He gave us all the spiritual resources and blessings necessary to live a Christian life that glorifies and pleases Him.

11. What are the three crowns specifically mentioned in the New Testament? List them, and then look them up and try to determine who is awarded these crowns in the corresponding Bible passages.

    Answer: (a) Crown of Life (James 1:12) – for the believer who endures temptation and for those who have loved Him; (b) Crown of Righteousness (2 Timothy 4:8) – for all who have loved (or longed for – NIV) Christ's appearing; and (c) the Crown of Glory (1 Peter 5:4) – for faithful pastors of God's flock.

Chapter Questions & Answers

Chapter 15

1. Does every believer automatically enjoy personal, daily "fellowship with God"?

   Answer: No, even though we may claim to be having fellowship with Him, we may be yielding to our sin natures and walking in sin.

2. Why do Christians fail?

   Answer: We fail as Christians by: (a) being proud and thinking our plans are better than God's; (b) being ignorant or neglectful of God's Word, the Bible; (c) walking in unbelief, believing the lies of Satan; (d) desiring God's will but depending on ourselves to accomplish it.

3. How does a believer "walk in the light" (1 John 1:7)?

   Answer: Through a willingness to walk by faith in the sphere of God's Word and truth, so that you have fellowship with God, which then results in the blood of Jesus Christ having a cleansing effect upon your spiritual growth and sanctification.

4. What does it mean to "confess" our sins (1 John 1:9)?

   Answer: It means to agree with God that what He says is sin, is indeed what we have committed in our thoughts, actions, speech, or motives.

5. Once we have confessed to God, what does He promise to do according to 1 John 1:9?

   Answer: He is faithful and just to forgive us our sins (the ones we have confessed) and to cleanse us from all unrighteousness (which includes the sins we have done ignorantly).

6. What is the purpose of our confession? (1 John 1:7)

   Answer: To yield to the Lord and walk by faith, and also to be restored to fellowship with Him again

7. What can we claim once we have confessed our sins to the Lord?

   Answer: God's total parental forgiveness

8. What happens if you refuse to believe your sins are forgiven after you confess them?

   Answer: You may scrutinize yourself constantly, become very sin-focused, or promise God you'll do better, or try to punish yourself, and hold onto your sins rather than becoming more Christ-focused.

9. What happens if you fail to confess your sins and cover them instead?

   Answer: You will walk in darkness, not have fellowship with God, and will not progress spiritually.

10. What does the Bible say that Jesus Christ does when Satan accuses you of sin?

    Answer: Jesus Christ defends you as your righteous advocate.

Chapter 16

1. What happens at the moment of physical death for the believer? (2 Cor. 5:6-8)

    Answer: At that very moment, you will be present with the Lord. There is no such thing as "soul sleep."

2. What will your body be awaiting upon death?

    Answer: Your body will be "sleeping" in the grave, awaiting the day that it is resurrected and reunited with your soul.

3. What could be stamped on the casket of every believer in Christ?

    Answer: "far better" (Phil. 1:23)

4. Why will there be a generation of believers in Christ that will never experience physical death?

    Answer: Because someday the Rapture will occur

5. What will happen "in the twinkling of an eye" to the generation of believers mentioned above?

    Answer: The Lord is going to catch up all living believers in Christ to meet Him in the air.

6. With what words should we comfort one another as believers?

    Answer: The words of 1 Thessalonians 4:13-18, which promise us that one day, whether we are alive as believers or have already died, we shall be caught up together with other Church-age believers to the meet our Savior, the Lord Jesus Christ, in the air at His coming for us. And then, we shall always be with the Lord!

7. When could the Lord Jesus come back to resurrect and glorify believers, and what should we be doing in light of this?

   Answer: He may come back to receive us at the Rapture any day—maybe even today; thus, we should be eagerly looking and waiting for Him to come at any moment!

8. How should we as believers view the Rapture in light of its description in Titus 2:13?

   Answer: We should view Christ's coming for us as our "Blessed Hope"!

GLOSSARY OF TERMS & DEFINITIONS

Advocate – one who defends another, usually in a courtroom scene

Apostasy – the turning away from sound doctrine or biblical truths

Apostles – specific leaders with ultimate human authority in the early Church who served under Christ's Headship

Begotten – one of a kind

Believes – personal trust, reliance or confidence in some object of faith

Beloved – a special object of God's love

Blessed hope – the blessed anticipation of Christ's future coming for church age believers at the Rapture

Blood of Christ – Christ's violent, sacrificial death upon the cross when He died to save us

Bodily transformation – the instantaneous process in which the believer's physical body will become like Christ's resurrected body in a glorified state

Born again – a spiritual birth from God that happens only once, the moment a sinner places his trust in Christ alone

Carnality – the state in which the believer is living under the dominating control of the sin nature or flesh

Chosen – that God has personally chosen and designed a special plan for you

Condition – a person's spiritual state in time

Confession of sin – the believer's honest admission to God of his sins in order to be restored to fellowship with God

Crowns – the analogy taken from athletic contests in which the victor receives a reward for finishing the race or winning the fight

Dispensations – successive divine economies during human history in which individuals are tested by God concerning their faith and faithfulness to the divine revelation they have received (They are not different ways of salvation.)

Divine viewpoint – a perspective that is shaped by the norms, standards, and principles of God's Word

Eternally secure – that one's eternal salvation can never be lost, forfeited, given back, etc.

Evangelistic – the desire or attempts to preach the Gospel to the lost

Evangelists – specific individuals who preach the Gospel, planted local churches, and equip others to evangelize

Everlasting life – a right relationship with God that will last forever

False doctrine – false teaching that does not correctly interpret or agree with God's Word

Fellowship – to have a joyful relationship and mutual compatibility/friendship with someone

The flesh – a synonym for the sin nature

Forgiveness – the divine releasing of the guilt of one's sins because of the blood of Christ

Glorified – to obtain a state of glory with God in Heaven that involves the absence of sin and presence of righteousness

Gospel – the good news from God of Jesus Christ and salvation through Him

Grace – God's unmerited or undeserved favor or blessing because of Who God is and what Christ has done

Great White Throne Judgment – the last judgment of mankind where all unbelievers will be judged by God for their unbelief in Christ resulting in every one being cast into the Lake of Fire

Heaven – a literal place of God's presence and total freedom from sin

Glossary of Terms & Definitions

Heavenly places – the believer's new realm of spiritual existence

Hell – a literal place of God's fiery judgment

Holy Spirit – the third person of the Triune Godhead whose ministries are important to every believer

Human viewpoint – a perspective that is shaped by the norms, standards, and philosophies of the world system

Imputing – an accounting term that describes the placing of a debt or asset to one's account

In Adam – the unbeliever's position or identity as viewed by God

In Christ – the believer's new position or identity as viewed by God

Intercessor – one who prays for another

Jesus Christ – the second person of the Triune Godhead who willingly became a man without sin to die for our sins and be raised from the dead to save us

Judgment Seat of Christ – the time following the Rapture in which Jesus Christ will evaluate the believer's post-salvation life to determine whether or not each one will receive a reward

Justified – to be declared righteous by God in His courtroom because of the finished work of Jesus Christ

The Law – the law given by God to Moses which includes the Ten Commandments

New nature – the nature received with the new birth which now has desires for the things of God

Oracles of God – the authoritative Word of God

Parental forgiveness – the specific forgiveness that God offers to His born-again children when they sin

Pastors – spiritual shepherds of God's flock who were to feed believers sound doctrine and oversee local churches

Peace of God – the believer's state of inner tranquility when he casts his cares upon the Lord instead of carrying his own burdens

Peace with God – the changing from a relationship of hostility to harmony because of Jesus Christ

Position – a person's spiritual standing before God

Positional forgiveness – the spiritual forgiveness God offers the unsaved when they place their faith in Christ

Powers – a term usually used also for angelic beings of a high rank like principalities

Prayer – communicating with God either mentally or verbally

Predestined – to predetermine the believer's destiny in Christ, namely to be "glorified" (Rom. 8:28-30)

Principalities – a term usually used for angelic beings of a high rank

Prodigal son – the son in Luke 15 who rebelled against his father, wasted his life and inheritance by indulging in sin, but eventually came to the end of himself by returning to fellowship with his father

Progressive sanctification – to be daily and progressively set apart to God from sin and the world in true holiness

Prophets – specific individuals who received direct revelation from God that was oftentimes predictive in nature

Rapture – the future event when both believers in Christ who've already died and believers who are still alive are resurrected and caught up to meet the Lord in the air to return to Heaven

Reconciled – to be brought into a right relationship with God through Jesus Christ

Redeem – to purchase out of a slave-market through the payment of a price

Redeem the time – to buy out of time the opportunities God gives you to serve Him

Retrogress – to backslide in one's spiritual state

Rewards – the recompense from God for faithfulness in the earthly lives of believers which determines each one's place of future, eternal service for the Lord

Saint – one who is set apart to God, thus a term for every believer since all believers are in the Holy One, Jesus Christ

Glossary of Terms & Definitions

Salvation – being delivered or rescued from some danger or peril to a state of safety or blessing

Sanctified – to be set apart unto God

Saved – to be delivered or rescued from the penalty for sin, which is eternal separation from God in Hell

Scriptures – another term for the Bible which consists of sixty-six divinely inspired books

Sin – the act, motive, word, or deed that is contrary to God's will and holy character

Sin nature – the naturally-born tendency or propensity to sin and rebel

Sound doctrine – healthy scriptural teaching based on the Bible

Spiritual blessings – the divine favors that have been bestowed upon every believer in Christ

Spiritual growth – the process of spiritual maturation that should occur after one is born again

Spiritually baptized – the believer is baptized or placed into union with Christ by the Holy Spirit at the moment of salvation

Spiritually dead – the unsaved are separated from God

Substitutionary death – Christ died in our place and for our sins

Supplication – to make an intense petition or request to God

Transformed – to be spiritually changed from the inside out

Trials – tests designed or allowed by God for the believer's good and spiritual growth to refine his faith

Unregenerate – the spiritual condition of all unbelievers who are without spiritual life in Christ

Verse-by-verse exposition – explaining the Bible verse-by-verse in its context in a systematic way

Walk – to conduct yourself step by step in a certain manner

World – while it may refer to the earth or its inhabitants, it is often used in Scripture to describe the world system controlled by Satan

Other Books & Booklets

If you found this booklet helpful, you may want to obtain other grace-oriented materials from Grace Gospel Press.

- *David: A Man after the Heart of God* by Theodore H. Epp. In this rich, biblical character study by the founder and first teacher of the Back to the Bible Broadcast you will get to know David—the shepherd, the songwriter, the warrior, the prophet, the king. You will learn why the Lord said concerning him, "I have found David the son of Jesse, a man after My own heart." Most importantly, you will learn about David's God and what it means to become a man or a woman after His own heart. (252 pp., softcover)

- *The Coming Kingdom* by Andy Woods surveys biblical teaching on the kingdom of God, showing that contrary to covenant theology and progressive dispensationalism, Jesus Christ did not set up a spiritual form of the kingdom at His first coming but instead the promised kingdom is still future. This book exposes how "kingdom now" theology has changed the focus of the church. (464 pp., softcover)

- *Disciplined by Grace* by J. F. Strombeck explains from Scripture how the Christian life in this present dispensation is designed by God to be lived entirely by His all-sufficient grace. Lewis Sperry Chafer said that this book "covers this ground and meets this need in a wonderful way. It should be read by every Christian. I commend it most heartily." Foreword by Warren W. Wiersbe. (154 pp., softcover)

- *Freely by His Grace* by 14 different authors covers the many biblical facets and themes related to God's grace, including faith, repentance, the Gospel, 1 Corinthians 15, Lordship Salvation vs. Free Grace, discipleship, regeneration, eternal security, assurance, sanctification, rewards, dispensationalism, discipleship, evangelism, and more. (634 pp., hardcover)

- *Getting the Gospel Wrong* by J. B. Hixson is a thorough explanation of the Gospel and salvation by grace alone through faith in the finished work of Jesus Christ. Several false forms of the gospel that are prevalent today in postmodern, American evangelicalism are compared and contrasted with the true, biblical standard of the Gospel. (324 pp., softcover)

- *The Gospel of the Christ* by Thomas Stegall is an in-depth, exegetical and theological response to the false teaching of the crossless gospel and the question of what a person must believe about Jesus Christ to possess eternal life. This book also serves as a valuable reference for correctly interpreting many difficult passages on the Gospel. (828 pp., hardcover)

- *The Judgment Seat of Christ* by Samuel L. Hoyt covers all major facets of this often neglected but imminent prophetic event. Originally written as the author's doctoral dissertation, the book is thorough yet easily readable and biblically balanced with a traditional dispensational, grace-oriented perspective. Foreword by John C. Whitcomb. (228 pp., softcover)

- *Must Faith Endure for Salvtion to Be Sure?* by Thomas Stegall clarifies the biblical view that eternal salvation does not depend on the believer's perseverance in faith and good works but on Christ's faithfulness and perseverance in keeping saved all who have trusted Him. (460 pp., softcover)

- *Repentance: The Most Misunderstood Word in the Bible* by Michael Cocoris surveys the use of the words "repent" and "repentance" in the Bible, resulting in a refreshing treatment of repentance that is based upon the authority of God's Word rather than religious tradition. (100 pp., softcover)

- ***Salvation in Three Time Zones*** by Dennis Rokser addresses the three tenses of salvation—one of the most vital and often misunderstood distinctions in the entire Bible. This book shows how the terms "saved" and "salvation" are used in Scripture and how God's grace guarantees the believer a past and future salvation, while also providing salvation in the present. Select "test" passages (Matt. 24:13; 1 Cor. 3:15; James 2:14-26) are thoroughly explained. (158 pp., softcover)

- ***Shall Never Perish Forever: Is Salvation Forever or Can It Be Lost?*** by Dennis Rokser shows how God's salvation is eternal, guaranteed, and cannot be lost. This book demonstrates from numerous Bible passages, with clear explanations and rich practical application, that one who has been genuinely born again is eternally secure and shall never perish forever, just as Jesus Christ promised in John 10:28. (362 pp., softcover)

- ***The Strombeck Collection*** by J. F. Strombeck is a collection of all five of Strombeck's classic books in one convenient volume, including *So Great Salvation, Grace and Truth, Shall Never Perish, Disciplined by Grace,* and *First the Rapture.* (608 pp., hardcover)

- ***Truthspeak*** by Michael Halsey sets the record straight regarding five key terms of the Christian faith, clarifying that "grace" does not mean works; "finished" does not mean incomplete; "repentance" does not mean do penance; "believe" does not mean commit, submit, yield, and obey; and "justified" does not mean guilty until proven righteous. An ideal book for showing people the difference between religion and God's grace and truth in Christ. (100 pp., softcover)

- ***10 Principles to Ponder When the Unexpected Happens: How Are You to Respond?*** by Shawn Laughlin offers hope from a biblical perspective. Trusting in Jesus Christ alone for eternal life guarantees a perfect hope (a certain future) in Heaven and this forms the basis for a hope while living on earth in all of life's uncertainties, even when life takes an unexpected turn for the worse. (24-page booklet)

- *A Tale of Two Thieves: Which Thief Describes You?* by Shawn Laughlin describes in an evangelistic way the account of Luke 23:32-43 and the two thieves who were crucified alongside Jesus Christ. As stated in the subtitle, readers will be challenged as to "Which Thief Describes You?" (19-page booklet)

- *Bad News for Good People and Good News for Bad People* by Dennis Rokser examines John 3:1-21 which is the most definitive passage in the Word of God that addresses the popular phrase "born again." (23-page booklet)

- *Grace Family Journal* is a quarterly journal available free by mail or online at duluthbible.org. (28-page journal)

- *Let's Preach the Gospel: Do You Recognize the Importance of Preaching the Gospel to Both the Unsaved and the Saved?* by Dennis Rokser explains 10 scriptural principles from 1 Corinthians 15 and the ministry of the apostle Paul regarding the need to preach the Gospel and its scriptural emphasis and content. Helpful for pastors, missionaries, and teachers. (57-page booklet)

- *Never Alone: From Abandoned to Adopted in Christ* by Becky Jakubek is her encouraging story of the grace of God! Left alongside a road in a shoe box as a new born, Becky gives her testimony of how she went from abandoned to adopted in Christ. (22-page booklet)

- *Planting & Establishing Local Churches by the Book* by Dennis Rokser is a biblical explanation of church planting designed to encourage the planting and establishment of indigenous local churches that glorify Jesus Christ by preaching and responding to the Gospel of God's grace—with all of its doctrinal and practical ramifications. (34-page booklet)

- *Promises of God for the Child of God* by Dennis Rokser provides the believer with some of the many promises of God found in His Word. The knowledge of God's Word and faith in God's promises are absolutely essential and delightful companions in every Christian's life. (39-page booklet)

- *Salvation in Three Time Zones* by Dennis Rokser explains from the Bible what it means to be "saved," showing that the term is used to describe three tenses of salvation for the believer in Christ—justification (past), sanctification (present), and glorification (future). This booklet also shows why distinguishing these three tenses is crucial for maintaining the Gospel of grace and correctly understanding the Bible. (42-page booklet)

- *Seven Key Questions about Water Baptism* by Dennis Rokser will help clear up one of the most controversial and confusing subjects in Christendom—water baptism. This booklet answers seven key questions on this subject from the Bible. (36-page booklet)

- *Seven Reasons Not to Ask Jesus into Your Heart: Answering the Question "What Must I Do To Be Saved?"*
by Dennis Rokser exposes one of the most often used but incorrect Protestant clichés of our day. Nowhere in the Bible is anyone ever instructed to "ask Jesus into your heart" to be saved. (52-page booklet)

- *The Need of the Hour* by Dennis Rokser presents a strong case for a return to preaching on the centrality of Jesus Christ with His supremacy and sufficiency, along with the verse-by-verse exposition of the Scriptures from a grace perspective. (12-page booklet)

How to Order

All *books* can be ordered from online retailers such as Amazon.com or Barnesandnoble.com. For *booklets* and all other material please visit us online at www.gracegospelpress.com or contact us at:

Grace Gospel Press
201 W. St. Andrews Street
Duluth, MN 55803
gracegospelpress@gmail.com
(218) 724-5914

CPSIA information can be obtained
at www.ICGtesting.com
Printed in the USA
BVHW091335110721
611330BV00001B/3